dining
in style

dining
in style

50 great hotel restaurants of the world

Madelin Wexler

HOTELS
The International Magazine of the Hotel and Hotel Restaurant Industry

Interior Details

AN IMPRINT OF

PBC INTERNATIONAL, INC.

Distributor to the book trade in the United States and Canada
Rizzoli International Publications Inc.
through St. Martin's Press
175 Fifth Avenue
New York, NY 10010

Distributor to the art trade in the United States and Canada
PBC International, Inc.
One School Street
Glen Cove, NY 11542

Distributor throughout the rest of the world
Hearst Books International
1350 Avenue of the Americas
New York, NY 10019

Library of Congress Cataloging–in–Publication Data

Wexler, Madelin
    Dining in style : 50 great hotel restaurants of the world /
Madelin Wexler and HOTELS
        p.   cm.
        Includes index.
    ISBN 0-86636-432-3 (hb : alk. paper). — ISBN 0-86636-477-3 (pb : alk. paper)
    1. Restaurants—Guidebooks. 2. Hotels—Guidebooks. 3. Menus.
I. Hotels. II. Title.
TX907.W474 1996   95-45407
647.95—dc20   CIP

CAVEAT– Information in this text is believed accurate, and will pose no problem for
the student or casual reader. However, the author was often constrained by information
contained in signed release forms, information that could have been in error or not included
at all. Any misinformation (or lack of information) is the result of failure in these attestations.
The author has done whatever is possible to insure accuracy.

Color separation, printing and binding by Dai Nippon Printing Group

Printed in Hong Kong

10 9 8 7 6 5 4 3 2 1

This book is

dedicated

to one who

has himself

experienced

fine dining

around the world,

my husband—

David S. Wexler

table of contents

foreword

I am proud that the majority of my 26 years as a chef have been spent within the magical world of hotels and their restaurants. Over the years, I have seen more and more great hotels, no longer content to offer just the classics, create wonderful new restaurants with unique characters all their own. Whether in Copenhagen at the Plaza, in New York at the Westbury, the Plaza Athenee, and Le Cirque (Hotel Mayfair) or now in my own Restaurant Daniel (adjacent to New York's Surrey Hotel), I have learned that fine cuisine is only one of the felicities guests insist upon. A hotel restaurant must appeal to all of the guests' five senses. It does so by making use of a chef's own five "senses": the graciousness of our **welcome,** the efficiency of our **service,** the authenticity of our **cuisine,** the selection of our **fine wines and spirits** and the warmth of our **ambience.**

Great hoteliers are realizing that guests are more attracted to restaurants with character, whether it be that of a great chef or a well-known restaurateur reputed for a unique sense of style and high standards. This scenario enables the restaurateur to offer a warmer **welcome** and to establish a meaningful and long term relationship with guests which will make them look forward to their next visit.

Providing the finest **service** means ensuring each guest that the staff will do their utmost to satisfy his and her every whim. In addition to being served in comfort with the greatest efficiency and discretion, a guest should be made to feel that almost any request will be accommodated. As **cuisine** and **wines** are a central attraction they must respect certain traditions yet remain spontaneous by following the rhythm of the seasons and the chef's creativity. Whether it be truffles, wild mushrooms or even seafood, highlighting seasonal harvests and unique local products brings character to a menu. A classic dish such as *Pheasant a la Souvarov* prepared for an entire table lends a festive air to celebrations, while a unique tasting menu paired with rare wines makes dinner itself a special occasion.

The **ambience** of the finest hotel restaurants is determined not by the latest design trends but rather the personal style and warmth of the chef and/or restaurateur. The perfect mix of casual sophistication can often be attained with just the right flowers and lighting.

It is only by constantly attending to each of these essential elements that a hotel restaurant can achieve the greatness that guests expect from it. As we continue to reinforce each "sense" as a crucial part of the whole, so will we continue to be appreciated by our guests from across the street and around the globe.

Chef Daniel Boulud
Restaurant Daniel, New York City

When you tell a friend or business associate that you just returned from a trip, the first questions are almost invariably "Where did you stay? Where did you dine?" Putting it simply, people *love* to talk about hotels and restaurants. They are a common experience that all of us can share, and comparing notes is one of the easiest and most enjoyable ways to get to know another person better.

In most parts of the world, the two experiences are combined because dining in hotels is synonymous with fine dining, and the restaurants in the great hotels have a reputation in their own right that is equal and sometimes even better than their host hotel's. In the United States, hotel dining does not have the same universal respect, but we do see hotel restaurants becoming more prevalent on all the annual "best restaurants" lists in the magazines and rating organizations.

Five years ago, we initiated an annual feature in our magazine that presents the best hotel restaurants of the world. Our goal was to acknowledge and encourage fine dining and to expand the public's awareness of great hotel restaurants. Our selections are not simply those of our magazine, but represent the collective choices of the best known restaurant critics and editors of hotel and restaurant magazines throughout the world.

The nominees for these annual awards and the selection committee were chosen by Madelin Wexler, a journalist with over three decades of experience in the hotel and restaurant field, including a number of years as editor-in-chief of our magazine. Madelin has traveled the globe throughout her career and is intimately familiar with the great hotels, hoteliers and restaurateurs associated with these restaurants. She is eminently qualified to produce this book.

Fine dining is a visual as well as a taste experience. Although we cannot reproduce every taste and every recipe that made these restaurants famous, we hope that you will enjoy this visual tour of some of the best hotels, and that we will encourage you to travel, visit and dine in some of the great hotel restaurants of the world.

Don Lock
Publisher, *HOTELS* magazine

introduction

With all the incredible restaurants in the world, why do famous gourmets, restaurant connoisseurs, and seasoned travelers focus so much of their time and energies on hotel restaurants? Because that's where the action is. That's where the greatest chefs go. That's where chefs have the opportunity to show their prowess in every aspect of food service and catering activities—banquets, buffets, room service and intimate private dining parties.

For years, there was an attitude that hotel dining was dull; guests seemed to prefer dining outside of the hotel. Not today. Hotels have set up restaurants that are unique, heavy with atmosphere or excitingly ethnic, to keep their guests "eating in."

Fantasy, imagination and culinary excellence combine to create one-of-a-kind dining experiences in these "Great Hotel Restaurants." For example, one of the most unusual restaurants in the world is a seafood extravaganza called Yü in The Regent Hong Kong where guests walk through floor-to-ceiling fish tanks, viewing brilliantly colored South Pacific specimens—all on the menu to be cooked as you wish, with the sauce of your choice. At the captivating Orient Express restaurant in the Taj Palace in New Delhi guests dine in an actual car from the famous train, and Morocco's exotic Le Marocain at La Mamounia creates mystery and romance with flickering Aladdin lamps and

Moorish arches. Additional unforgettable atmosphere restaurants visited in *Dining in Style* include the charming *Out of Africa* bistro Relais du Parc in Paris's Le Parc Hôtel, and The Conservatory, the handsome domed dining museum with an Oriental collection amid lush greenery in London's Lanesborough hotel.

But one does not dine on decor alone. Examining new trends in food is an essential part of this book. The most obvious development over the past years has been to make "Fantasy Food." It grew out of nouvelle cuisine, but today the portions are larger. The art still stars: edible flowers and outlandish garnishes distinguish the plates worldwide, making presentations highly impressive. Particularly the appetizers and desserts are inspired creations—colorful, delicate and whimsical. Almost too pretty to eat.

Dining in Style exposes the techniques of clever chefs and the ways they please their customers. Although French cuisine is clearly the dominant style of cooking throughout the world, the young chefs of today cannot resist combining it with unexpected flavors and exotic foods.

What is initially important to most of the 50 great chefs, and especially the new breed, is that their food tastes good without an abundance of high calorie ingredients. Several important chefs are decidedly anti-sauces, including

Dominique Le Stanc at Le Chantecler in Nice's Hôtel Negresco, and Alain Ducasse of Le Louis XV in Monte Carlo, who says with conviction that "Sauces are out."

Light cuisine is an important goal for many of our chefs. In London's Four Seasons restaurant, Jean Christophe Novelli features the hotel chain's "Alternative Cuisine." At the Hotel Bel-Air in Los Angeles, the *cuisine legere* menu is the choice of many patrons, and at The Conservatory, Chef Paul Gayler always offers tempting vegetarian dishes and stresses salads.

Increasingly appearing is the Asian influence. Combining French and Pacific Rim flavors is especially noticed at Lespinasse at New York's St. Regis, and in the menus of Jeff Tunks at New Orleans's Grill Room in Windsor Court, (40 percent of the sales in that room are Chinese Smoked Lobster). Wolfgang Von Wieser of The Regent Melbourne's restaurant uses local game but combines it with Thai or Chinese foods.

Almost all of our 50 great chefs pride themselves on having set up their own sources of produce and local products. They all embrace freshness as their religion, so seek purveyors who will put fresh ingredients at their fingertips. The word "fresh" is sacred to these professionals who contact their suppliers daily to be sure that their pears or snow peas or haricot vertes will be available for tomorrow's menus.

Emphasis on local foods, of course, means there are authentic ethnic menus in our collection. Harald Schmitt, veteran chef of Nassauer Hof's Orangerie in Wiesbaden, believes that preparing simple regional cuisine of Germany is his mission, so he sticks faithfully to the foods of the immediate area.

Another development: more chefs are writing daily menus. Many have specials, to be sure, but the young lions today want to be creative and experiment with new tastes and fanciful recipes in order to please demanding clientele.

The "Greats" have been chosen over a period of six years—ten per year—by a team of experts gathered by *HOTELS* magazine, the world's only international hotel journal. Each year the 20-member selection committee is asked to vote for ten restaurants from a list of 100 submitted to them by the editors of *HOTELS*. Authorities such as George Lang, author and owner/operator of Café des Artistes (New York's most popular restaurant), Patricia Wells, food editor of the *International Herald Tribune*, and Robin Leach, host of television's *Lifestyles of the Rich and Famous* and *Talking Food*, have told us why they consider these restaurants "great." Always alluring atmosphere, fine food and superb service combine to define "great."

Madelin Wexler

THE st. giorgio

Superb Italian cuisine fits Venice's paradisical island hotel

The Cipriani's motor launches bring guests across the lagoon from San Marco Square. Outdoor dining offers vistas across gardens and water.

For a meal at the Hotel Cipriani—in the famous St. Giorgio—one takes a thrilling ride in the hotel's private launch. It picks up visitors in front of the Piazza San Marco and speeds them across to the idyllic island hotel.

One could hardly expect a commonplace dining experience in this beautiful spot. In the 1960s the Cipriani served a daring new dish, Carpaccio Classico, a first course "invented" for a banquet to honor the Carpaccio Centenary (an exhibition of artist Carpaccio's work). Now the dish is internationally famous.

St. Giorgio gained its fame due to founder Commendator Giuseppe Cipriani, an extraordinary restaurateur who won acclaim for Harry's Bar in Venice. His dream was to create a private hotel near the heart of Venice. He acquired three acres on a nearby island and in 1958, two years later, the hotel and restaurant were flourishing.

After Cipriani retired in 1976 the hotel was sold to Mr. Jim Sherwood who hired one of Europe's

On the lovely little island of Giudecca, surrounded by lagoons, the Cipriani is a lush, secluded resort. It has the only swimming pool in Venice.

The dining room off the central circular room provides party space and is used for extra seating on busy days.

most prestigious hoteliers to maintain the country house atmosphere.

Dr. Natale Rusconi, former manager of Rome's Grand Hotel and Venice's Gritti Palace, and his staff are dedicated to personalized service and fine food. Rusconi attracts heads of state, and international VIPs.

Parisian architect Gerard Gallet contributed largely to the success of the Cipriani with his interior design of the main dining room with its elegant pink vaulted ceiling and luxurious draperies.

Renato Piccolotto, the 41-year-old *chef de cuisine* who started at the St. Giorgio in 1970, creates

the menus. He began his career in 1971 at the Villa Cipriani in Asolo, Italy where he was trained by the famous Cipriani.

Seats: 88
Serving: lunch & dinner
Covers sold: 100 (more in summer)
Service staff: 36
Kitchen brigade: 18
Check average: L100,000 (US$68.75) without beverages
Market composition (guest origins): American 35%, British 32%, French 15%, Italian 10% (30% are repeat customers)
Opened: 1958; redecorated in 1979
Affiliations: An Orient-Express Hotel, The Leading Hotels of the World, Relais & Chateaux
Photography by Mark Mogilner

FROM THE MENU

Fresh green noodles with
ham au gratin—L37,000 (US$23)

Rosettes of veal Cipriani with
marsala wine, black truffles, fresh
mushrooms, gruyere cheese—
L56,000 (US$35)

Sautéed scampi with tomato/caper
sauce and curried pilaf rice—
L63,000 (US$39)

*At The St. Giorgio in Venice's
Hotel Cipriani, views of waterways
and beautiful islands with magnificent
architecture entrance guests dining
on the chef's Venetian specialties.*

*Three outdoor terraces used for dining—in a garden, poolside and on
the lagoon—provide the serene beauty for which the Cipriani is noted.*

THE mansion on turtle creek restaurant

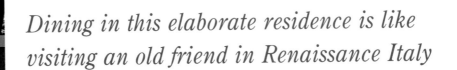

Dining in this elaborate residence is like visiting an old friend in Renaissance Italy

Left abandoned and in disrepair during the 1970s, the magnificent old Sheppard King Mansion in Dallas's fashionable Turtle Creek residential area greatly interested Caroline Rose Hunt. As founder of Rosewood Hotels & Resorts she set about acquiring it for the company.

This lovely old symbol of Texas high society became the five-star Mansion on Turtle Creek hotel and restaurant, restored and decorated by Hirsch/Bedner & Associates, and Vision Design, inspired by Mrs. Hunt's refined taste.

Stanley Marcus of famed Neiman-Marcus says, "The Mansion has an ambience that all restaurateurs and decorators try to achieve—an intangible sense of euphoria."

Service at the Mansion is incomparable—the ratio of staff to guests is three-to-one. This contributes largely to its

16

On entering the foyer one sees that the magnificent Italian Renaissance-style mansion (owned in the 1920s by Sheppard King) was meticulously renovated.

Red jalapeño Caesar salad with shrimp diablo "tamale," is a lively, colorful offering.

being honored so often by critics, magazine surveys and guides.

Such notables as the queen of England and Presidents George Bush and Bill Clinton have enjoyed the Southwest cuisine prepared by The Mansion's Executive Chef Dean Fearing. He creates 24 new dishes

each week. Inspired by the backyard barbecues he knew as a child, he recently presented rack of wild boar with watermelon glaze and basil mashed potatoes.

After a classical culinary education, Fearing worked in famous restaurants, then opened his own, Agnew's, which was acclaimed by Craig Claiborne of *The New York Times.* Fearing's daring Southwest food experiments brought him the prominence which led to his becoming The Mansion's executive chef.

Grilled swordfish with its three sauces (mango, black bean and red chili) is a festive, flashy and delicious dish.

Seats: 135
Serving: lunch & dinner
Kitchen brigade: 46
Opened: 1981
Affiliations: Rosewood Hotels & Resorts, Preferred Hotels & Resorts Worldwide, Small Luxury Hotels of the World
Photography courtesy of The Mansion on Turtle Creek

FROM THE MENU

Tortilla Soup—US$8.50

Mansion Red Japanese Caesar Salad with Shrimp Diablo "Tamale"—US$14

Warm lobster taco with yellow tomato salsa and Jicama salad—US$17.50

Grilled swordfish with Mexican fried pasta salad and three sauces: black bean; mango; and red chili—US$30

Pan-roasted ostrich filet and chili-corn tamale with smoked shrimp enchilada, red bean mousse and wild huckleberry sauce—US$40

The main dining room surrounds guests with a dazzling array of artwork and exotic accessories. The glow from arched windows illuminates the carved gilt ceiling.

THE black forest

An arresting doorway to The Black Forest provides entrance directly into the enchanting little restaurant.

This charming little restaurant is filled with color, crafts, whimsy and great German food

The Black Forest is a tiny, quaint dining spot in the grand old Brenner's Park-Hotel & Spa. Hotel guests love the relaxed room with its decor so typical of the Black Forest area. It is a comfortable alternative to the elegant Park restaurant in the hotel.

The Black Forest has, in addition to its hotel guests, a loyal following from Baden-Baden. Approaching the picturesque cafe is part of the fun, for Brenner's Park-Hotel is located in a private park facing the renowned Lichtentaler Allee and the river Oos. For over 120 years an international clientele has gathered here to enjoy Brenner's ambience, gourmet dining and regional specialties.

Master Chef Albert Kellner has an impressive background, having worked throughout Europe. Born in Bavaria, he received his training and apprenticeship in Munich.

Red pom-poms on bright white lamps add a cheerful note while playful cuckoo clocks and clown faces delight. Bright red candy-striped curtains and red Bavarian-print upholstery on old-fashioned carved chairs all make it a treat to eat in this charming place designed by architect Professor Caesar F. Pinnau.

Seats: 35
Serving: lunch & dinner
Service staff: 4
Kitchen brigade: 4
Opened: 1970
Affiliations: The Leading Hotels of the World, Preferred Hotels & Resorts Worldwide, Relais & Chateaux
Photography by Rolf Gottwald Fotodesign

An intricately carved cuckoo clock is one of the whimsical objects of art that adorn the forest green walls of The Black Forest.

20

Playful and picturesque, the cozy Black Forest dining room lures guests who enjoy exquisitely prepared German foods and fairy-tale ambience.

FROM THE MENU

Turbot on tomato fondue with basil sauce—
DM56 (US$40)

Saddle of venison with juniper cream and
mushroom ragout, homemade spaetzle
and apples gratinée—DM60 (US$43)

Ice cream soufflé Stephanie with raspberry sauce
—DM22 (US$16)

Saddle of venison with juniper cream and mushroom ragout.

21

truffles

Whimsical boars and high iron gates are unique, wonderful trappings

One enters the winsome, airy world of Truffles through hand-crafted iron gates and is greeted by striking artworks, the most unexpected of which are the wild boar sculptures that play up Truffles's name and menu specialties.

For years Truffles was Toronto's prime award-winning restaurant—the only Canadian one that ranked in the top 25 hotel menus of America. Now it has won the distinguished Five Diamonds from the Canadian/American Automobile Association just as the hotel won for 12 years.

It was interior expert Rosalie Wise Sharp who boldly transformed Truffles into its present

A truffle-hunting Uffizi boar guards the entrance. This happy creature was created by Canadian wood-carver Christina Luck.

glory after it had been called "stuffy and too much like a hotel restaurant." She followed the hotel's policy of using local artists and craftsmen to create original objets d'art for the public rooms.

Chairs are alternately of light cowhide and dark velour; the centerpiece is a mosaic floor inlaid with 11,000 pieces of exotic woods. The remaining floors of Truffles are padded with custom-made Irish Axminister carpeting.

The wide columns are scalloped along the corners and have niches to hold sculptures. The entire interior glows from the maple wood paneling throughout.

A Frenchman, well educated in culinary arts, Xavier Deshayes, began as chef in 1994 at Truffles after gaining intense experience in California at the San Ysidro Ranch, Santa Barbara and Citrus Restaurant in Los Angeles, then as sous chef at the Four Seasons, Beverly Hills.

Iron gates crafted in the technique of a blacksmith provide dramatic entrance.

Seats: 80
Serving: dinner
Service staff: 11
Kitchen brigade: 9
Check average: CDN$52
(US$38)
Gross annual sales: CDN$1.4
million (US$1.02 million)
Market: 80% local
Opened: 1993 (renovated and
remodeled)
Affiliations: Four Seasons◆
Regent Hotels & Resorts
Photography courtesy of Four
Seasons Hotel

*Artwork in a lighthearted interior
makes dining interesting. Designed
by Rosalie Wise Sharp, the restaurant features a wood mosaic floor
and supporting columns with
niches for sculptures.*

FROM THE MENU

Spaghettini with Perigord black gold, truffle
emulsion sauce—CDN$15 (US$9.75)

"Mouclade of the Sea," saffron chardonnay
stew of lobster, shrimp, scallops, clams, and
mussels—CDN$30 (US$19.50)

Oven-roasted rack of veal, yam and Yukon gold
potato risotto, grain mustard sauce CDN$32
(US$20.80)

THE grill room

An English-style grill with a diverse cross-cultural menu

The highest standards of service and style are found in the Windsor Court. And for food, The Grill Room is enormously popular, serving haute cuisine in a quiet, refined atmosphere. It is so popular, in fact, that even hotel guests make reservations weeks in advance of their stay. Subdued lighting and soothing classical music, amply cushioned armchairs and heavily draped tables make The Grill Room comfortable and appealing.

The interiors of the hotel are both old-world elegance and contemporary design, incorporating an exceptional collection of art and furnishings, including works by Gainsborough and Reynolds.

Executive Chef Jeff Tunks brings new flavors to The Grill Room's old favorites. Tunks's signature dish is Chinese smoked lobster, accounting for 40 percent of The Grill's sales. He built a reputation in his previous position with Loews Coronado Beach Hotel in the Azzura Point restaurant, called the "hottest place in San Diego," by the *Los Angeles Times*.

The Grill Room's many honors were earned over the past years by Kevin Graham, a bright young chef who left to start his own restaurant. Jeff Tunks sticks to Graham's high standards but adds more seafood, Asian influences and southwest cuisine. He also teaches in the Windsor Court's Cooking School.

Seats: 148
Serving: breakfast, brunch, lunch & dinner
Gross annual sales: US$2.9 million
Opened: 1984
Affiliations: An Orient-Express Hotel, The Leading Hotels of the World, Preferred Hotels & Resorts Worldwide
Photography by Eugenia Uhl

One little corner with an eighteenth-century Brussels tapestry, and floral upholstery sparks the private dining room—The Board room.

Modeled after the famous Grill Room at London's Savoy, the restaurant provides a stately setting for the grand cuisine served. Interiors are by Frank Nicholson.

Shape, texture and color combine nicely in this stunning plate presentation.

WINDSOR COURT HOTEL

FROM THE MENU

Turbot with summer vegetable scales and blood orange tarragon butter—US$35

Ono Ebi: sweet Hawaiian red shrimp with seasonal salad and toasted peanut vinaigrette —US$12.50

Sorbet Leonardo da Vinci: layered sorbet with fruit and a cookie spiral—US$8.50

THE causerie

An intimate little refuge in London's busy Mayfair

"Causerie" is from the French word *causer*, to chat, or have an informal discussion. Certainly this is the place for that, and has been since World War II when it first attracted senior British and Allied officers.

Causerie's atmosphere is a blend of tearoom and cocktail lounge, with a celebrated centerpiece—the appetizing smorgasbord with countless dishes rimming a round table.

The smorgasbord is priced three ways depending on which type of drink is ordered with it. This unusual pricing came about during the war when the Causerie was first created in 1942, just after rationing had been introduced. Throughout the war the hotel was unable to charge adequately for any food consumed. Instead guests were charged for their drinks and ate free.

Combining tailored banquettes and Scandinavian lounge chairs keeps the restaurant casual, while finely set tables with pink napery suggest a high level of cuisine. Full luncheon and dinner menus are the creation of Marjan Lesnik, 45, who became the maitre chef of Claridge's and The Causerie in 1984. For culinary excitement, he mingles French haute cuisine with his own Slovenian influences.

A splendid old London landmark, dating back to 1812, Claridge's was acquired by The Savoy Group in 1894 and rebuilt in 1898.

Seats: 50
Serving: lunch & dinner
Service staff: 9
Kitchen brigade: 7
Gross annual sales: £315,000 (US$500,000)
Affiliations: The Savoy Group, The Leading Hotels of the World
Photography courtesy of The Savoy Group

FROM THE MENU

Fricassee of plaice and mussels with fresh pasta and saffron—£11 (US$18)

Salmon délice in a potato crust with basil sauce—£13.50 (US$18)

Poached filet of beef with herb pasta—£19 (US$30)

Chicken curry with basmati rice, condiments and poppadom—£14.50 (US$23.75)

Lime Soufflé—£6.50 (US$10.25)

Opposite: The cozy Causerie offers table d'hôte and á la carte in addition to the abundant delicacies on the smorgasbord.

relais du parc

*A bistro at last!
After all the
elaborate
restaurants in
Paris, this relais
is a joy to know*

Delightful and whimsical, Relais du Parc also has its own kind of refinement and luxury. It is not formal, nor is its cuisine, but the quality of the furnishings and food is evident. Designer Ferré Duthilleul based the design for Relais du Parc on a motif from the film *Out of Africa.*

Located in an exclusive section between L'Arc de Triomphe and the Trocadero, near the Eiffel Tower, Relais is situated behind the historical facades of five buildings encircling the courtyard. The deluxe hotel, renovated in 1992, is decorated in an English style.

Joël Robuchon, the owner and proprietor of the three-Michelin-star restaurant, "Joël Robuchon," is director and consulting chef to Relais, as well as being in charge of the hotel's room service. His restaurant is in a restored private mansion linked to Le Parc Hôtel.

Although Robuchon has entrusted Relais's cooking to the highly capable *Chef de Cuisine* Gilles Renault, he often

In summer, Relais extends its seating into the courtyard, which is surrounded by the hotel's five vintage buildings.

A corner table reflects the colonial ambience with its intriguing memorabilia to titillate diners

helps compose the menu and pops in from across the courtyard to taste a new dish. The seasonal menu may include a pumpkin soup served in its shell and a mandatory copper pot of Robuchon's famous mashed potatoes which the French dignify as potato pureé.

Seats: 75
Serving: breakfast, lunch & dinner
Covers sold: 190 (daily)
Service staff: 17
Kitchen brigade: 15
Check average: FF254 (US$53) including beverages
Gross annual sales: FF15,052,884 (US$3,131,000)
Market: 30% hotel guests, 70% local
Opened: 1992
Affiliations: Demeure Hotels International, the luxury division of Compagne International Phoenix (CIP Hotels)
Photography by Charlie Erwin

NEWSPAPERS

One of the two dining rooms in Relais du Parc is decorated in an Out of Africa *theme.*

FROM THE MENU

Book sausages with mashed potatoes—FF107 (US$22)

Veal stew in white sauce with spring vegetables—FF107 (US$22)

Roast duck with turnips—FF192 (US$40)

Fine apple tart with cinnamon ice cream—FF49 (US$10.20)

In Relais du Parc guests enjoy a charming setting while watching chefs prepare hearty bistro dishes.

le cirque

Le Cirque means "the circus," and the ringmaster runs a great show

It is the people who make this restaurant spin. The patrons (many of them rich and famous), the waiters, the chefs, the kitchen crew, but mainly it's the owner Sirio Maccioni, an Italian who learned the kitchen and the ropes at Maxims in Paris, then worked in top hotels in Europe, and finally came to New York.

Though Le Cirque is next door to the Mayfair Hotel, on East 65th Street, it is a separate enterprise, one started in 1974 when the part-owner and manager of the hotel, William Zeckendorf, Jr. invited Maccioni to open his own restaurant just to the right of the hotel entrance.

Having this popular, dedicated restaurateur "in" the hotel was a coup for Zeckendorf because it brought people to the hotel and eliminated the need to open a posh dining room.

Maccioni had almost instant success in his small but glowing 28-table dining spot. He had come to know celebrities and powerful business people during his years at The Colony where the wealthy, celebrated crowd gathered. He easily lured them to his new place and they have been loyal for decades.

No signs of a circus theme surface in Le Cirque's decor. It is restrained and of obvious quality, but the unexpected elements are the monkeys.

Chef Sylvain Portay took over the kitchen in 1992. With ample experience under French and Italian culinary experts, he worked four years at Louis XV, one of the "Great Hotel Restaurants," before coming to Le Cirque.

FROM THE MENU

Sea scallops in black tie—US$22 (appetizer), US$36 (main course)

Lobster Risotto—US$18 (appetizer), US$28 (main course)

Paupiette of black sea bass with braised leeks and red wine sauce—US$31

Braised veal shanks with Swiss chard, tomatoes, scallions and black pepper—US$33

Crème Brulée Le Cirque—US$9.75 (Paul Bocuse borrowed this recipe, gives credit on his menu)

Seats: 108
Serving: lunch & dinner
Covers sold: 350 (daily)
Check average: $100 (including beverages and tax)
Gross annual sales: $5 million
Opened: 1974
Affiliations: The Leading Hotels of the World
Photography by Jerry Ruotolo

Above: The crowded tables are approved by many. "Enforced intimacy is an essential part of the atmosphere... nearness to celebrities is an ego-massage," says one critic.

Left: An astonishing element in Le Cirque's dignified decor is the monkey. Life-sized figures watch patrons and muted murals with monkeys playing actively adorn the walls. Interiors were designed by Ellen McClusky.

35

le louis XV

The richness and pomp of Louis XV is in the decor and table settings

Graphically delightful, this brochure is typical of the good taste and originality that emanate in menus and greeting cards.

Alain Ducasse, the dynamic young chef of Le Louis XV, is changing the face of French cooking. He believes in simplicity, freshness, true flavors. "It's what people want to eat today. The last thing they want is something heavy, dripping in sauces. Sauces are finished!"

This tack is quite a contradiction to the ornate and lavish restaurant itself with portraits of Mesdames de Pompadour and du Barry looking upon the gilt-edged furnishings and wealthy clientele.

At age 33 Ducasse became the youngest chef in history to earn three stars from Michelin. In 1986 he signed a contract with the glamorous Hôtel de Paris guaranteeing three Michelin stars within four years to retain his position. To achieve such an honor from the gastronomic bible of France in 33 months is miraculous as it usually takes a new restaurant a decade to win three stars.

Ducasse has organized the whole restaurant with imagination and a perfectionist's eye. For example, the dining room crew irons the cloths on the tables, and even the dishes are unique. The silver-gilt underplates are signed by Louis XV, and the plates were chosen and signed by the chef.

For dessert, the tables are entirely redecorated with blue, white and gold, including napkin rings and candlesticks.

Seats: 60
Serving: lunch & dinner
Covers sold: 50 (lunch), 60 (dinner)
Service staff: 22
Kitchen brigade: 20
Gross Annual sales: US$3.75 million
Affiliations: Societé des Bains de Mer Hotels, The Leading Hotels of the World, Tradition et Qualité
Photography courtesy of Hôtel de Paris

FROM THE MENU

Vegetables from the gardens of Provence simmered in black truffles with Ardino olive oil, balsamic vinegar and fine sea salt—FF321 (US$66)

Local fish cooked whole with green tomatoes, sliced Menton lemon and chick-pea pancakes—FF361 (US$74)

Louis XV dessert: pastry of ground caramelized almonds—FF136 (US$28)

Heavily gilt-edged, the decor of Le Louis XV fits the opulence of his period, but is far more elaborate than the new, simplified cuisine served.

kable's

Photo by Paul Torcello

Unique Australian food in a sleek atmosphere

A few steps away from Sydney's glittering harbor and opera house, on the second level of The Regent, the city's food cognoscenti converge on Kable's. First-rate cuisine and an appealing ambience attracts them to the hotel's celebrated restaurant.

Guests enjoy spacious dining rooms with handsome Australian interior style—from the Tasmanian timbers to the vibrant paintings by Patrick Hockey, one of the country's world-renowned artists.

The restaurant takes its name from Henry Kable, a convict who arrived with the first fleet. Despite his poor start back in England, Kable became Australia's first jailer at the prison built in 1796 on The Regent Sydney site. He prospered as one of the colony's leading merchants.

Executive Chef Serge Dansereau has created a cuisine dubbed "haute Australian" by food critics. Dansereau describes it as "an intelligent style of cooking which uses Australian food and products with sophistication."

The best chefs, Dansereau feels, maintain a direct line from kitchen to grower. This encourages producers to aim for quality and develop new foods. And there are many, for example: Llabo lamb, bug tails, Coffin Bay scallops, Wapengo Lake oysters, local morels and marrons.

Kable's serving staff, formally attired, are friendly, bright, discreet people who understand the food they serve.

Seats: 114 (including private dining room)
Serving: lunch & dinner
Covers sold: 75-90 (lunch), 65-110 (dinner)
Service staff: 13
Kitchen brigade: 32
Check average: A$53 (US$39.50) lunch including beverages, A$76 (US$57) dinner including beverages
Market: American, European & Japanese leisure travelers
Opened: 1983
Affiliations: Four Seasons◆ Regent Hotels & Resorts, The Leading Hotels of the World
Photography by George Seper, Paul Torcello

Sofas and banquettes, highlighted with navy and terra-cotta, have distinct Japanese overtones. Photo by George Seper.

Steamed Western Australian snapper fillet with coriander mousse and bok-choy leaves, with virgin olive oil. Photo by George Seper.

Mango flan accompanied by pineapple sherbet. Photo by George Seper.

Tartar of oysters and salmon with osietre caviar. Photo by George Seper.

40

Pan roasted squab breast with Asian mushrooms and shallot confit. Photo by George Seper.

Right: The wine cellar has a remarkable collection of Burgundy, Bordeaux and Rhone, as well as a dazzling variety of Australian wines. Photo by George Seper.

Mellow and warm, the spaciousness of Kable's makes patrons feel important. Tasmanian woods and rich fabrics spell elegance. Photo by George Seper.

FROM THE MENU

Wok-seared flakes of ocean trout, water spinach
& chestnuts—A$24 (US$18)

Kobe beef raised in Australia—A$27 (US$20)

Antipasto of rock fish, scampi and yabbie tails—A$16 (US$12)

Layers of lime mousse, banana roulade with sautéed banana,
coconut sauce—A$12 (US$9)

yü

Many may consider this a great "fish story," but Yü's seafood extravaganza really does exist

As guests enter the shining, contemporary restaurant Yü at The Regent Hong Kong, they are surrounded by enormous curved fish tanks set into the walls displaying the wide choice of exotic fish offered on the menu.

To further enlighten guests about these colorful swimmers, hand-painted fish cards accompany the menu. The cards identifying the exciting Southeast Asian fish are mounted in a handsome canvas holder. Each fish is named in Chinese, Latin and English.

Interiors are bold and modern with a distinctively aquatic theme. Designed by Hirsch/Bedner & Associates, the restaurant has a light, casual feel that emphasizes the connection between the harbor waters and the aquaria. Glass is used extensively to reflect and enhance the feeling of water and space.

The seawater tanks themselves were custom-made in New Zealand. To provide the proper environment for fish from a wide variety of international waters, several different tanks were installed. A water purification system using no chemicals was set up in each tank, as were temperature and light controls.

"Every effort is made to maintain the sea environment," says Executive Chef Jürg Blaser who explains that the water itself is deionized purified drinking water with salt from the Red Sea. Chef Blaser is in charge of all five of The Regent's restaurants—three of which are described in this book—Lai Ching Heen, Plume and here, Yü, the novel, comfortable dining experience.

Silver starfish and crab napkin rings reflect the seafood cuisine.

Seats: 94
Service: lunch & dinner
Covers sold: 120 (lunch & dinner)
Serving staff: 20
Kitchen brigade: 15
Check average: HK$740 including beverages (US$93.50)
Market: 65% local (80% Chinese, 20% Westerners), 20% hotel guests
Opened: 1993
Affiliations: Four Seasons◆ Regent Hotels & Resorts
Photography by Peter Seaward

Fish from the South China Sea swim in tanks with scientifically controlled seawater to keep them fresh. Patrons select fish which are prepared immediately.

Maori

芝 麻 班

Coris lineolatus

Mandarin Fish

桂 魚

Siniperca chuatsi

Western Star Garoupa

西 星 班

Plectropomus maculatus

43

Yü's informal, modern dining room has beautiful woods and leathers, inlaid tables and a lovely view of Hong Kong harbor.

Yü's paella features grilled chicken and seafood.

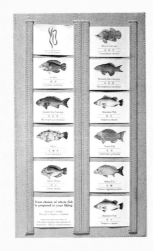

FROM THE MENU

The Regent Seafood Platter: seafood on ice with six sauces. The selection depends on the market, but usually is composed of lobster, yabbies, jumping shrimps, king prawns, oysters, red shell scallops, clams and mussels for two—HK$680 (US$88.50)

Yü Paella, Spanish saffron rice with sautéed vegetables, grilled chicken filets and grilled seafood—HK$180 (US$23.50)

Sautéed Boston lobster with black beans and fine noodles—HK$295 (US$38.50)

Steamed live fish from the South China Sea, Chinese style with soya sauce—market price

Yü ice soufflé, a cold dessert that appears to be a hot soufflé—HK$78 (US$10)

The seafood platter at Yü is bountiful, with a variety of shellfish depending on what is fresh at the market. It is offered in three sizes for two, four or six.

The bubble wall astounds guests entering Yü, the seafood restaurant in The Regent Hong Kong.

lai ching heen

H een also means "happy and laughing" as well as "balcony or pavilion." All these apply to this marvelous Chinese restaurant voted one of the best in the world by Patricia Wells, the traveling food editor of the *International Herald Tribune* and a renowned cookbook author.

Situated on the Kowloon waterfront with its nautical pageant of ships, junks, yachts and fishermen, The Regent's Chinese restaurant has glass window walls so guests see a colorful drama by day and the twinkling lights of Hong

delicate green of the table settings. These traditional soft tints suggest tranquillity. At the entrance is a seventeenth-century Zi Tan table with flowers of the current Chinese lunar month. The menu is also changed every new moon.

Chef Cheung Kam Cheun, an artist with Cantonese cuisine, worked his way gradually through the intricate hierarchy of the Chinese kitchen in many fine restaurants and hotels in Hong Kong before joining The Regent in 1980. It had no Chinese restaurant, so his first four years there he headed the Chinese kitchen which catered to the large and prestigious banqueting operations.

By 1984 Lai Ching Heen opened and Chef Cheun gathered a first-rate kitchen team of creative, quality-minded people who helped him reach the top of Chinese culinary circles.

Lai Ching means "The Regent Hotel" in Chinese while Heen means "elegant dining establishment"

Hand-carved spoons and napkin rings are jade; chopsticks are ivory with silver, and napkins are Swiss linen.

Kong at night.

Lai Ching Heen is beautiful in its simplicity. Table settings are the focal point. Presentation plates, napkin rings, curved spoons and carved chopstick stands are all handcrafted in green jade, a symbol of excellence and purity. The chopsticks are ivory and silver.

Colors in Lai Ching Heen are rose and pale gray to complement the

Serving: lunch & dinner
Covers sold: 260
Service staff: 40
Kitchen brigade: 24
Check average: HK$350 (US$45.25) lunch; HK$700 (US$90.50) dinner
Market: 30% Japanese; 40% local; 30% American, European and hotel guests
Opened: 1984
Affiliations: Four Seasons◆ Regent Hotels & Resorts
Photography by Peter Seaward

Simplicity and tranquility characterize this room with oriental pires inside and out. Critics say it's the best Cantonese restaurant in the world.

At the entrance to Lai Ching Heen are flowers symbolizing the Chinese lunar month. They decorate the menu, the tables, fruit platters and finger bowls.

Deep-fried scallops with pear is a favorite dish. (left) Double boiled imperial bird's nest is served from a whole coconut.

FROM THE MENU

Deep-fried scallops with pear—
HK$130 (US$16)

Roast whole chicken
Lung Kong style—HK$300 (US$36)

Double boiled superior sharks fin with
bamboo piths—HK$380 (US$49)

Braised asparagus with crab roe
HK$167 (US$21.60)

Luscious roasted Lung Kong chicken is offered in whole or half portions.

plume

**THE REGENT
HONG KONG
KOWLOON**

Drenched in candlelight, this French dining nirvana offers enthralling views

Plume has been winning accolades for more than 10 years for its incredibly fine food and wine. In The Regent Hong Kong, where it competes with two other "Great Hotel Restaurants" —Lai Ching Heen and Yü —its popularity does not diminish. Seldom can diners experience this delightful package: unwavering service, superb specialties from France and Italy, and an immense view of Hong Kong's skyline.

When The Regent was built Plume occupied two floors—ground floor and first floor. In 1993 the new seafood restaurant Yü took over the upper floor making Plume more intimate but still the premier restaurant in the hotel.

The one page menu consists of four composed dinners, one of which is the Plume Classics (next page), the others are Seafood, Mediterranean and Summer. Thomas Axmacher, general manager of The Regent was highly impressed by Hubertus Cramer's culinary expertise and style when he met the talented chef in Munich in 1994. At the age of 30 Cramer became Plume's *chef de cuisine*. Trained in Germany and France at Michelin-star restaurants, Cramer is happily adding foods and Pacific seafood to his classics. He describes his cuisine as "light and modern combining traditional and new recipes with local market-fresh ingredients."

Seats: 98
Serving: dinner
Covers sold: 80
Serving staff: 20
Kitchen brigade: 18
Check average: HK$1,100 (US$142)
Market: 60% local, 40% hotel guests & tourists
Affiliations: Four Seasons◆ Regent Hotels & Resorts
Photography by Peter Seaward

A stylish addition to Plume is a bijou-like private room and wine cellar made with crackled glass. Its surfaces reflect the glittering scene in a kaleidoscopic way.

FROM THE MENU

Plume

Delicate cream of artichoke soup—
HK$110 (US$18)

Gooseliver parfait with Perigold truffles—
HK$231 (US$30)

Lierbed rack of lamb on bean ragout with
polenta—HK$347 (US$45)

Poppy seed strudel on white chocolate and
plum sherbet—HK$110 (US$1

Right: Baby artichokes with uncommon relishes.

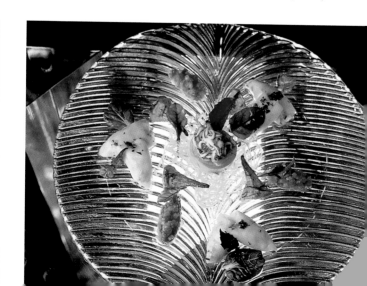

postrio

*Imagine, three
executive chefs!
If one is
Wolfgang Puck
the food is
bound to be a
continuing
success*

In a city where superb restaurants are the rule and patrons are mostly gourmets, Postrio is an enduring favorite. The excitement generated by the menu results from the combined energies of Wolfgang Puck (the renowned Los Angeles chef whose fame began with Ma Maison and Spago) and the brothers Rosenthal, Steven and Mitchell.

The name results from the restaurant being located on San Francisco's Post Street and because it is run by a trio of chefs. Situated in The Prescott Hotel, Postrio is actually a tenant, not owned by the hotel or its parent the Kimpton Group. Bill Kimpton, the head of the 24-unit hotel chain believes in finding the very best restaurateurs and inviting them to give guests the very best in dining. Room service in the hotel is also handled by Postrio.

Designed by a daring restaurant specialist, Pat Kuleto, Postrio is contemporary American design accented by modern art. A striking colored ribbon pattern in the carpet and on the marble floors ties the three levels together visually and reflects the design influence of Puck's partner and wife, Barbara Lazaroff, acclaimed restaurateur and designer. Custom lighting includes 3-foot-diameter hanging orbs with ribbon-patterned supports.

A large exhibition kitchen adds action to the main dining room, and a wood-burning pizza oven and grill operate in the bar. The cuisine is Puck's interpretation of San Francisco foods with Asian and Mediterranean influences. The menu changes daily emphasizing local products.

Seats: 180
Serving: breakfast, lunch & dinner, brunch on weekends
Covers sold: 150 (lunch), 340 (dinner)
Service staff: 100
Kitchen brigade: 85
Opened: 1989
Affiliations: Kimpton Hotel & Restaurant Group
Photography courtesy of The Prescott Hotel

Postrio, in The Prescott Hotel, produces off-beat pizza and a host of fascinating, exotic dishes invented by Wolfgang Puck and his two chefs.

postrio
SAN FRANCISCO

Left: Copper handrails and accents unite the three-leveled space.

FROM THE MENU

Home-smoked Beluga sturgeon with a trio of horseradishes and potato pancakes—US$12.50

Spicy Moroccan sausages with eggplant white fig compote—US$10

Sautéed calamari with herb linguine and sweet curry sauce—US$12.50

Grilled veal T-bone with marble potatoes, baby fennel and shallot glaze—US$26

Crispy fried Wolfe ranch quail with spicy greens and pineapple glaze—US$20.50

51

THE orient express

Bon voyage and bon appétit! greets guests

An exact replica of the luxurious Orient Express restaurant car is located within the posh Taj Palace, one of India's most opulent hotels.

To reach The Orient Express, guests enter the "station," a cocktail lounge where the full-sized dining car is located. While waiting for a table, patrons find great enjoyment watching the diners through the windows and observing the lavish service.

Every detail of the romantic Orient Express has been duplicated under the supervision of interior designer Elizabeth Kerkar.

Even the tabletop items such as china, glassware, cutlery and lovely peach linens have been reproduced. The overall effect is polished and elegant.

The restaurant menu is inspired by the cuisine of all the countries through which the Orient Express travels, and a map of the fascinating route from Venice to London adorns the lively menu cover.

At the remarkable age of 32, Executive Sous Chef Shivanand Kain is in charge of The Orient Express kitchen, assuring that the finest quality food is served. He has been with Taj Hotels for more than nine years after training in some of London's

FROM THE MENU

Scottish smoked salmon with herbed cream cheese and salmon roe—Rs375 (US$11)

Grilled scallops with a red bell pepper sauce—Rs443 (US$13)

Four course dinner: Main course—New Zealand lamb chops on vegetables julienne, with rosemary flavored juice —Rs1,602 (US$47)

finest kitchens. Though skilled in Indian and Chinese cuisine, his specialty is continental with a serious French flair.

Right: Making the set more realistic, porters with luggage ply the "station," people enter and leave the car, and elegant waiters go in and out.

Seats: 36
Serving: lunch & dinner
Covers sold: 10 (lunch) 34 (dinner)
Service staff: 11
Kitchen brigade: 10
Market: International business travelers and tourists
Check Average: US$29 without beverages
Opened: 1983
Affiliations: A member of the Taj Group of Hotels
Photography by Peter Hopkins

Dinner in the replicated Orient Express dining car is a "trip" in itself as it transports guests to the grandeur of the belle époque style of the old train.

le marocain

A genuinely exotic adventure awaits guests dining in this Moorish haven at the glorious Mamounia

Le Marocain is an elaborate and palatial restaurant with intriguing Moroccan cuisine prepared by a chef who was trained with all women in the Pasha's Marrakech Palace. The menu, written in Arabic, French and English indeed does offer delights fit for a pasha.

Tangines, spicy North African stews are the most typical foods of the region and appear on the menu in many forms but most often with lamb. Le Marocain's chef, Boujemaa Mars, has been at the hotel since 1962. He travels all over the world as an ambassador for Moroccan food, explaining it, teaching the techniques and attracting potential patrons to come to Marrakech and dine in the magnificent restaurant.

Designed in 1922, La Mamounia's architects combined art deco elements and traditional Moroccan style. It was expanded and completely refurbished in 1986 by architect Andre Paccard. Commenting on the dazzling and ornamented interiors of Le Marocain, Paccard said that here "Too much is not enough."

The hotel is set in a two-century-old garden, (usually referred to as a park), covering seven acres with unusual, luxuriant flora. Some of the vegetables served in the hotel's restaurants are grown in the park's garden, and oranges and olives from the park's trees are used as well. Guests can stroll through the gardens and see the variety of items grown. Not just the flora makes the park a joy to visit but a marvelous variety of birds and butterflies inhabit the gardens.

Moorish architecture with all its carving, arches, and marble provides a splendid setting to sample the cuisine of Marrakech.

Seats: 120
Serving: dinner
Service staff: 14
Kitchen brigade: 20
Market: 70% hotel guests, 10% local
Opened: 1987
Affiliations: Leading Hotels of the World, Concorde Hotels
Photography by Mr. Alain Gerard

Low Morrocan sofas and tables are set among delicately tiled walls and columns, marble inlaid floors, in an authentically designed Moroccan interior.

FROM THE MENU

Couscous with spring lamb and seven vegetables
out of the hotel's gardens—DH251.70 (US$30)

Tangia Marrakchia, lamb shank cooked in earthenware jar,
the specialty of Marrakech—DH251.70 (US$30)

Steamed shoulder of lamb for two—DH500 (US$60)

THE
THE LANESBOROUGH
LONDON
conservatory

*Glass-domed and bursting with lush greenery,
this marvelous room dazzles diners with exotica*

The Lanesborough, on Hyde Park corner, combines classical and Greek-revival style of the Regency period.

The Conservatory and the splendid Lanesborough hotel could only happen once in a century. Consider the team that conceived of, financed, renovated and decorated this London masterpiece. Rosewood

The Lanesborough's grand entrance hall replicates the work of nineteenth-century architect William Wilkins.

Hotels & Resorts Inc. is the operating company, carrying out the wishes of the wealthy owners, the royal family of Abu Dhabi.

With these resources, Julian Reed of the highly respected interior design firm Ezra Attia & Assoc., and Michael Woodcock of Fitzroy Robinson & Partners, created a monument. Everyone involved in the project became so obsessed with details of the neoclassic/late-Georgian period that they

Chinese figures copied from England's Brighton Pavilion add to the ambience of The Conservatory.

asked the Royal Fine Arts Commission, The Georgian Society, the Victorian Society and English Heritage to supervise, insuring authenticity. All the furnishings were carefully researched. For example, the design for the Chinese-motif carpet in The Conservatory was found in eighteenth-century archives.

The epicurean delights in The Conservatory are the work of Executive Chef Paul Gayler whose menus feature light salads, enticing appetizers and his renowned vegetarian dishes. Gayler began his culinary career auspiciously—he worked with Anton Mosimann at the Dorchester in 1980. Seven

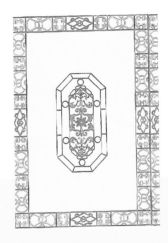

(Prices include service and tax)

Lettuce spring rolls with spicy crabmeat—£9.50 (US$14.25)

Thai lobster risotto—£19.50 or £24.75 (US$29.25 or US$37)

Tagliatelle of wild mushrooms and spring vegetables—£9.25 (US$14.50)

Filet tournedos of beef (in its own juices), potatoes—£22.50 (US$33.75)

Capuccino brule—£5.95 (US$9)

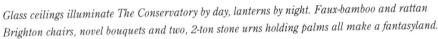

Glass ceilings illuminate The Conservatory by day, lanterns by night. Faux-bamboo and rattan Brighton chairs, novel bouquets and two, 2-ton stone urns holding palms all make a fantasyland.

years later he was Mosimann's deputy. Then he was lured by the famed Inigo Jones restaurant. He joined The Lanesborough when it was opened New Years Eve 1991.

Traditional tea is served all afternoon with piano music. An à la carte menu and two set tea menus are offered, the more costly includes champagne. In the evenings dinner guests enjoy the resident pianist and three nights a week festive supper dances are held.

Seats: 106
Serving: breakfast, lunch, tea, dinner and after-theater supper
Covers sold: 250 (daily)
Service staff: 30
Kitchen brigade: 31
Check average: £21 (US$33) including beverages
Opened: 1991
Market: 60% American
Affiliations: Rosewood Hotels & Resorts Inc., Preferred Hotels & Resorts Worldwide
Photography by Klein & Wilson

Afternoon tea is prettily served in a perfect setting. Designer Julian Reed says, "We wanted a light feeling here so we chose colors like icing on a cake."

THE grill room

No one cares about a table with a view, guests all come to watch celebrities, or each other

It is a lovely room, traditional and cheerful, but the decor is not the draw. At The Grill, it is the prestige of being there, and the excellent cuisine, dubbed by Chef David Sharland as "a blend of nouvelle and classical—what the customer wants."

And over the century that tack has been carefully followed. The Savoy Grill's Maître Chef Auguste Escoffier created dishes for Sarah Bernhardt, Lily Langtry, and the Prince of Wales.

The Savoy and Grill Room were opened in 1889 by Richard D'Oyly Carte (of Gilbert & Sulli-van fame). In addition to Escoffier, he invited Cesar Ritz from Paris to be the general manager thus setting unequivocally high standards for every aspect of the hotel and its restaurants.

The history of The Grill is peppered with astonishing incidents. The Queen Mother, in an unheard of gesture for royalty, stood to applaud Maria Callas when she arrived for supper after her great Tosca opening. During WWII after a bomb blew the stage out, Noel Coward

Round tables in a separate room make the tablecloths flow gracefully and give more flexibility.

Chef David Sharland proudly displays his terrines and pâtés.

strode through broken glass to the piano and gave one of his greatest performances.

And this is the place where Lawerence Olivier met Vivien Leigh, and where Cary Grant came to rediscover sausages and mash. The Savoy Grill records the history of dining in Britain. What other restaurant would hold table number four, Winston Churchill's, for a year after he died?

Manager Angelo Maresca is the current key to The Grill's public relations success. He is at the door greeting peers and politicians and steering them discreetly to their tables. Says Maresca to his staff, "You must make *all* your clients feel at home, whoever they are, not just the regulars."

Seats: 85
Serving: lunch & dinner
Covers sold: 85 (lunch),
120 (dinner)
Serving staff: 24
Kitchen brigade: 18
Affiliations: The Savoy Group,
The Leading Hotels
of the World, Utell
Photography courtesy
of The Savoy

THE SAVOY
in 1650

GRILL ROOM

FROM THE MENU

Omelette Arnold Bennett—£11 (US$17.50)

Salad of pan-fried Dublin Bay prawns, bacon, avocado and lettuce leaves—£18.50 (US$30)

Duck liver terrine with an orange-scented brioche—£19.50 (US$31)

Filet of veal with braised sweetbreads on onion puree with leeks and Girolle mushrooms—£18.95 (US$30)

The tables along the wall with comfortable banquettes seem to be favorites of cabinet ministers and newspaper editors. The classic interiors are light and cheerful.

Finely designed but casual, the cheerful Orangerie pavilion with its warm colors and ample windows are reminiscent of a refined country summerhouse.

HOTEL NASSAUER HOF
WIESBADEN

orangerie

An inviting greenhouse ambience is a sunny refuge
for guests at Hotel Nassauer Hof

A more traditional decor in some sections reflects the hotel's 170-year landmark status.

I n the cold climate of Wiesbaden, Germany, a bright dining room such as Orangerie's offers a warm haven where guests can enjoy authentic and traditional dishes of Germany. The culinary glory of the Orangerie is due primarily to Harald Schmitt, the restaurant's head chef and manager, and the hotel's food and beverage manager. A believer in serving the best food and wines of the region, he says, "When traveling, I don't want the same cuisine in Hamburg as in Munich.

"It's a challenge to me to transfer great cuisine with its elegant, expensive products to simple German regional cuisine," continues Schmitt. "That means pike perch instead of *loup de mer*, or farm-cock instead of *bressse poulard*." Schmitt is assisted in his creative mission by two fine chefs, Klaus Weingartz and Andreas Haugg.

The glowing interiors of the Orangerie were designed by Ilse v. Beckh, Jutta Babock and Barbl Kachele. The colors naturally fit the name, and the furnishings were skillfully chosen to be dignified, yet still relaxed. The upholstery fabrics and carpeting are tailored with a contemporary flair, and contrast beautifully with the gold and peach walls and sparkling chandeliers.

Comfortable chairs of timeless rattan give the pavilion an informality compatible with foliage murals and greenery. White napery and shining crystal welcome guests to a dining atmosphere that is truly *gemutlich*.

Seats: 100
Serving: breakfast lunch & dinner
Covers sold: 92 (lunch), 120 (dinner)
Service staff: 26
Kitchen brigade: 28
Affiliations: The Leading Hotels of the World, Preferred Hotels & Resorts Worldwide
Photography courtesy of Hotel Nassauer Hof

Tender baby Chicken with mushroom sauce and pike-perch turnovers stuffed with tartar of salmon (right).

THE dining room

Ritz-Carltons worldwide call their restaurants simply "The Dining Room"

In Atlanta's most gracious neighborhood, just ten minutes from downtown, the Ritz-Carlton hotel boasts a Dining Room that has won the hearts of its gourmet guests as well as the AAA Five Diamond award six years consecutively. It was also voted Atlanta's best by four different publications.

The restaurant has a refined, residential atmosphere with comfortable silk upholstered seating and museum-quality art on mahogany walls. Soft lighting, exquisite flowers and classical background music complete the ambience. Skilled interior designer Frank Nicholson has consistently created appealing residential decor for this and many of the Ritz-Carltons.

For culinary excitement, Chef Guenter

Shrimp candies on lentil ragout.

Seeger creates European haute cuisine with American regional overtones, writing different menus daily, based on what fresh items his suppliers can deliver. His meticulously prepared food is matched by fine wines selected by Master Sommelier Michael McNeill.

Seeger's culinary interest started in Germany where his parents had a wholesale produce business. He learned early the importance of fresh ingredients. In 1977 he started his own restaurant near the Black Forest which was soon recognized as one of the best in West Germany. Soon after he received a Michelin star. In 1985 he brought his expertise to The Dining Room in Buckhead.

Though fixed price menus are suggested, Seeger offers an à la carte menu for guests to create their own four-course dinner, at the same price. The flawless service is handled by a professional, tuxedoed wait staff.

Seats: 80
Serving: dinner
Service staff: 12
Kitchen brigade: 8
Opened: 1984
Maître d': Peter Krehan
Market: 60% local clientele
Affiliations: Ritz-Carlton Hotels, The Leading Hotels of the World
Photography courtesy of The Ritz-Carlton Buckhead; John Grunke

The Dining Room is set for those who appreciate quality: satin damask upholstery, original paintings and the famous Ritz blue goblets. Photo by John Grunke.

FROM THE MENU

Fixed Price Dinner—US$58 without beverages; US$86 including wines

Salmon Carpaccio Fennel and roasted bread
   (1994 Nachenheimer Rottenberg, Riesling
   Kabinett Reinhessan)

Loup de mer (sea bass), avocado *mousseline,* sweet
pepper compote and summer truffles
   (1991 Marrietta's Well, Livermore Valley)

Summerfield veal sirloin, braised romaine,
foie gras sauce and fried noodles
   (1992 Ladioux, Les Chaillots Merode, Burgundy)

Warm chocolate cake in mint sauce and
marinated blackberries
   (1994 Moscato di asti, St. Stefano, Piedmonte)

THE restaurant at the bel-air

This sybaritic hideaway is just minutes from bustle and action

The graceful swans add romance to this idyllic setting. No ordinary hotel, the 92 rooms are located in separate, mission-style villas.

Nestled within a heavily wooded canyon, surrounded by 11 ½-acre estate grounds, The Restaurant at the Bel-Air seems a very private place. Still, diners in search of fine French-California foods and a poetic scene readily find this nirvana, just one mile west of Beverly Hills.

Gary Clauson, executive chef at the Bel-Air since 1992, has brought unceasing creativity to the menu. For those who prefer light food, he introduced *cuisine lègére* with minimal fat and reduced calories.

In connection with the opening of the Hotel Bel-Air's Fitness Center, Chef

The bougainvillea-covered terrace with its heated stone floors provides year-round alfresco dining.

Clauson rolled out a new spa menu available in the restaurant as well as for room service. Clauson took select dishes from the appealing Bel-Air menu and lowered calorie, fat, cholesterol and sodium levels. The spa menu lists the nutritional value of each entrée which is computed by a software program.

Interior design in the Bel-Air restaurant is a challenge because of the fine line between casual and formal. Due to the resort nature of the hotel, with its gorgeous grounds and swimming

In contrast to the open, California look of the restaurant, the hotel bar is traditional and richly paneled with wood.

pool, guests often resist dressing up; business people meeting for breakfast or lunch follow the California custom of no ties, yet at night a formality is recognized. Designer Jerry Beale of Wilson & Associates has accomplished this blend of beauty and comfort with panache. Touches of velour and leather reflect quality but not opulence.

Seats: 90 (restaurant), 60 (terrace)
Serving: breakfast, lunch & dinner
Covers sold: 100 (breakfast), 120 (lunch), 150 (dinner)
Check averages: US$15 (breakfast), US$25 (lunch), US$50 (dinner without beverages)
Gross annual sales: US$7.5 million
Opened: 1946
Affiliations: The Leading Hotels of the World, Preferred Hotels & Resorts Worldwide
Photography by Mary Nichols

FROM THE MENU

Veal medallions with crayfish risotto, spinach timbale and crayfish sauce—US$30

Peppered filet of Angus beef, Maui onion tart, horseradish potatoes and patty pan squash—US$32

Orecchiette pasta with smoked duck and mushrooms, wilted arugula and peas—US$22

Encompassed by flowers and exotic greenery, the Restaurant at Hotel Bel-Air embodies comfort and beauty with just a touch of formality.

restaurant haerlin

This deluxe dining room, facing a lovely lake, retains its century-old reputation as Germany's finest

For almost 100 years the Vier Jahreszeiten and its formal Restaurant Haerlin have pleased the most knowledgeable connoisseurs of fine food and beautiful interior design. The room is furnished with tapestries, antiques, comfortable period chairs, light creamy faux-marble walls, and sparkling chandeliers—a marvelous atmosphere cheerfully illuminated by day through wide lake-front windows, and by candlelight in the evenings.

The most celebrated features of the room are the century-old porcelain sculptures of nymphs symbolizing the four seasons (the translation of Vier Jahreszeiten).

Service in Haerlin is fastidious, by a staff that is trained to perform flawlessly. Impressive silver gueridons are used for table service so waiters can serve hot foods directly with lavish personal attention.

A formal dress code is observed in Haerlin and for the tourist who comes unprepared, tie and eye glasses can be loaned. In the evenings guests enjoy piano music.

The menu is in German, English and French and all dishes are available in half portions. This custom was begun by the famed founder Friedrich Haerlin who understood that some guests have smaller appetites.

The *Chef de Cuisine* Hans-Gunther Harms prepares dishes that vary with the seasons—special lobster, white herring asparagus and venison. Harms experience was mainly in Northern Germany—at the Atlantic Hotel, the Landhaus Scherrer (famous for its nouvelle cuisine), and the Intercontinental Renaissance. He joined Vier Jahreszeiten in 1992.

Seats: 70
Serving: breakfast, lunch & dinner
Year restaurant opened: 1897
Affiliations: The Leading Hotels of the World
Photography by Uwe Aufderheide

Lighted from windows facing Alster Lake, Haerlin features antiques and comfortable chairs, but most important are four porcelain statues representing the seasons.

FROM THE MENU

Prix fixe dinner DM 205 (US$145)

Gelée of wild pigeon

Sole in leeks and truffles

Sweetbread ravioli with trevisano

Selection of cheeses

Nougat pear with red wine

la rotonde

Only the Swiss could meld such fine cuisine, flawless service and idyllic views for pure dining delight

This enchanting old world hotel, the Dolder Grand, seems right out of a fairy tale. Within the city of Zurich it has its own golf course on the lake.

La Rotonde (a befitting name for the lovely rotunda) is a deluxe restaurant within the Dolder Grand Hotel. La Rotonde has been famous for more than 70 years, while the hotel itself is more than 120 years old. The view overlooking the lake, mountains and gardens is enjoyed by both those within the dining room and guests on the Garden Terrace.

The menu itself is unique in that one side lists carefully prepared traditional dishes while the other offers seasonal foods. The French and Swiss specialties are masterfully handled by Chef George Angehrn, born and educated in the United States. After college he attended Hotel Management School Belvoirpark and later joined the Dolder Grand in 1975. He was made *chef de cuisine* in 1989.

Lively is the word for La Rotonde. Every Wednesday evening a

Luncheon or tea on The Garden Terrace is pleasurable and peaceful. As the profusion of crystal indicates, the hotel serves extensively from its celebrated wine selection.

74

Inside, its formal grandeur surprises guests and makes them feel like royalty in such a palatial marble hall.

Left: Richly paneled, with an antique patina, the bar is a comfortable gathering place.

FROM THE MENU

Finely sliced veal filet in a white wine and parsley sauce—Fr. 47 (US$42)

Fillet of John Dory fish fried with asparagus, potatoes and truffles—Fr. 60 (US$52)

Lobster (fresh from the aquarium) in sauce with dill—Fr. 66 (US$58)

Grilled calf's kidney with horseradish and mustard—Fr. 36 (US$32)

Salmon from Ireland or Norway, cured and smoked—Fr. 30 (US$58)

76

A handsome silver and wood trolley reveals a tempting array of hors d'oeuvres. in the Dolder Grand's dining room.

candlelight dinner is held with live background music. After a concert on Sundays, a special meal is presented: an hors d'oeuvres buffet, then the main course from the menu, followed by a dessert buffet.

Visiting chefs stimulate both guests and staff. This year's *Semaine Culinaire* hosted Jean-Pierre Bruneau from Brussels. Every year there are Burgundy & Bordeaux Wine Weeks when special menus are created and each course is accompanied by a specific wine.

Seats: 150
Serving: breakfast, lunch & dinner
Covers sold: 100 (lunch & dinner)
Service staff: 35
Kitchen brigade: 45
Opened: 1924
Gross Annual Sales: US$2.5 million (food & beverage)
Market: 30% hotel guests; 70% local, private banquets, business meetings
Affiliations: The Leading Hotels of the World, The Swiss Leading Hotels
Photography by Stephan Knecht, Langnau

With a spacious air and golden glow, La Rotonde's uncovered windows afford breathtaking views of mountains, lakes and forests.

A display of delicious desserts delights patrons who appreciate both the variety and excellence of the offerings.

club del doge

Imagine, breakfast on the Grand Canal! Between the sublime Palace and fine food, it is a thrilling set

Maybe the food in Venice simply tastes better because it is such a magical place, maybe the seafood really is very different, maybe the chefs are superior because they compete so fiercely. In any case, cuisine in Venice has a unique character.

The Club del Doge's cuisine, like its architecture and paintings has been influenced for centuries by the Middle East. But it remains faithful to the genuine freshness of fish from the lagoon and produce from gardens on the little islands in the estuary. Local recipes are foremost in Chef Celestino Giacomello's mind as he creates the menus.

One of the specialties is Sfogi saor, Adriatic baby soles, fried in oil, marinated in saor (onions, white wine, vinegar, sugar, raisins and pine kernels) served cold with hot polenta and grappa.

The noble palace was home of Venice's hero, the 77th Doge of Venice, Andrea Gritti, a merchant, warrior and statesman who built great churches and palaces.

But the history of Venice is not all that dignifies Club del Doge. Famed author Somerset Maugham wrote fondly: "There are few things in life more pleasant than to sit on the terrace of the Gritti when the sun, about to set, bathes the Church of the Salute in lovely colors.

"At the Gritti you are not merely a number . . . you are a friend who has been welcomed when you sit down to dinner at the very same table you sat at the year before, and the year before that, and you see your bottle of Soave in the ice pail waiting for you, you cannot but feel very much at home."

Seats: 80 (inside), 60 (terrace)
Serving: breakfast, lunch & dinner
Affiliations: ITT Sheraton The Luxury Collection
Photography by Gian Mauro Lapenna

Luxuriantly furnished with brocade fabrics, marble floors and wainscoting, Club del Doge is fit for royalty.

Ristorante Club del Doge

FROM THE MENU

Pasta and bean soup, Venetian style—L25,000 (US$15.75)

Risotto with scampi and zucchini—L35,000 (US$22)

Braised fillet of sole with vegetables—L45,000 (US$29)

Steamed calamari with celery, cucumbers and eggplant cream—L30,000 (US$19)

Overlooking the Grand Canal with the Church of the Salute and colorful gondolas in sight, the terrace of Club del Doge is an enthralling dining locale.

Indeed a setting for a nobleman and his lady, gorgeously appointed yet refined and genteel

Here is the splendor of the nineteenth century with all its grand trappings. Burgundies, crimsons, rusts, and pinks on paisley patterns create a breathtaking setting.

In a restaurant such as Le Gentilhomme even a business lunch turns into a memorable occasion, while a supper or dinner dance gives the impression of a grand ball as the bar never seems to close.

Exquisite cuisine, vintage wines from as far back as 1875, the specialty of caviars, brandies and cigars all testify to the luxurious traditions of the restaurant.

One of Europe's highly experienced and respected hotel families, the Armleders, have for four generations maintained the high standards of this lovely place.

Here nothing is left to chance. The beauty of a flower arrangement and the freshness of a butter pat are considered equally important as the proper functioning of crystal lighting sconces and chandeliers.

With the exclusiveness of a private club and the drama of a theater, Le Gentilhomme is the perfect retreat for le gentilhomme.

Gloriously rich in burgundies, rusts, and reds, Le Gentilhomme has the refined air of a gentlemen's club.

Seats: 30
Serving: lunch & dinner
Service staff: 8
Kitchen brigade: 14
Check average: SFR117 (US$100)
Opened: 1987
Affiliations: A Concorde Hotel, The Leading Hotels of the World, Preferred Hotels & Resorts Worldwide
Photography courtesy of Le Richemond

1875

FROM THE MENU

Loup de mer (sea bass) cooked over coarse salt for two—SFR20 (US$18) per 100g

Rack of lamb roasted in a blend of chopped parsley and garlic for two— SFR84 (US$75)

Lobster salad with peaches—SFR32 (US$28)

le

gentilhomme

la mer

*Halekulani means "house befitting heaven,"
and dining in La Mer is a sublime interlude*

With all the density and commotion on Waikiki beach, the beautiful legendary Halekulani is clearly an isolated paradise. It occupies five acres on the beach and extends out into the water so that its view of the striking mountain, Diamond Head, is one of the best in Honolulu.

La Mer benefits from this fortunate site as it has a lovely view of the mountain and is situated over the sea so the rhythmic sound of the surf is the loudest music one hears. The interior atmosphere of La Mer is unlike any restaurant. Its richness and simplicity depend on the teak paneling and soft gold oriental paintings. The curled brass trim frames each window and alcove, while ample rattan dining chairs with their lively fabric are inviting and comfortable.

But this wonderfully romantic mood is matched by some of the region's most inspired cuisine, produced under Executive Chef George Mavrothalassitis. The Marseilles-born chef known as "Mavro" trained with many greats in France—Allen Senderens and the Troisgros brothers to name a few.

Mavro won the Gault Millau Best of Hawaii (Restaurant Food) with a 17/20 rating, and has won the AAA Five Diamond Award five years in a row. Further to Mavro's

A serene enclave on busy Waikiki, The Halekulani is a gracious resort whose alluring restaurant La Mer occupies a breeze-cooled upper floor of the main building. Photos by David Franzen.

Papillote of Kumu with basil, seaweed, mushrooms. Photo by Eugene Kam.

credit, he has won many other honors from surveys and publications over the seven years that he has been in command of La Mer's cuisine.

Seats: 90
Serving: dinner
Covers sold: 80
Serving staff: 12
Kitchen brigade: 16
Check average: US$100
Gross annual sales: US$2.9 million
Opened: 1985
Affiliations: The Leading Hotels of the World, Preferred Hotels & Resorts Worldwide, Okura Hotel chain
Photography by David Franzen, Eugene Kam, Camera Hawaii

Salt-crusted onaga (red snapper with herbs). Photo by Eugene Kam.

FROM THE MENU

Yellowtail tuna in a salad of cucumber, tomatoes, mint—US$25

Spicy Ahi Sevruga caviar and fried taro wafer—US$20

Red snapper baked in a crust, sauce of fine herbs—US$41

Goat fish baked with seaweed, Maui onions and shitake mushrooms—US$41

Mango Tatin Tart with licorice ice cream—US$12

Warm pineapple with pineapple and coconut sauce—US$12

Mango Tatin Tart with licorice ice cream. Photo by Camera Hawaii.

Overlooking the water, La Mer's teak-walled interiors recall a tranquil Buddhist temple. Photo by David Franzen.

cafe pierre

In a stately hotel on Fifth Avenue, one can expect such a great cafe

Entering Cafe Pierre is like going into a Gallic haven where you encounter award-winning food.

86

The Pierre is a prominent historical landmark on a busy corner. Inside Cafe Pierre diners enjoy serenity and beauty. The cafe resembles the reception room of a neoclassic French chateau. Decorated in tones of pale yellow and gray with silver accents, the cafe is embellished with Italian gray marble inlaid with gilt-edged bronze, etched Italian mirrors, imported silks and satins, and trompe l'oeil wall and ceiling murals.

Designed by Valerian Rybar, Cafe Pierre displays the same fine qualities as the famed Pierre hotel has since its opening in 1930—a European grace and elegance, attention to detail and flawless service.

Interestingly enough this hotel was preceded by its restaurant, Pierre's on Park, built by Corsican emigrant Charles Pierre Casalasco in 1904. Completed much later, in 1930, the posh hotel fell into bankruptcy, but was revived by Jean Paul Getty in 1938. Hiring Frank Paget as general manager, Getty's wish that The Pierre would be the nicest hotel in New York was realized. ("It's the only thing I have above the ground," said Getty.)

Restaurant Chef Bertrand Vernejoul creates seasonal menus with dishes that reflect his light, modern approach to classic cuisine. Throughout the menu, bright little stars indicate the Four Seasons's Alternative Cuisine: low calorie, low fat, high nutrient.

Cafe Pierre's wine list has been given the prestigious "Best of Award Excellence" by The Wine Spectator. Another magazine praising Pierre's way said, "The food is beautifully presented, impeccably served and paced in such a way that you can enjoy."

Seating: 54
Serving: breakfast, lunch & dinner, pre- and post-theater dinners & suppers, Sunday brunch
Covers sold: 180 (daily)
Service staff: 15
Kitchen brigade: 15
Check average: $47 (dinner)
Gross annual sales: $1.7 million
Opened: 1930
Affiliations: Four Seasons◆ Regent Hotels & Resorts, The Leading Hotels of the World
Photography by Jaime Ardiles-Arce

Cafe Pierre with its muted marbles, bright brass and warm yellows provides New York's aristocracy with a genteel yet lively refuge.

FROM THE MENU

Risotto with wild mushrooms, asparagus, truffles and chervil—US$13

Warm terrine of roasted eggplant, red pepper, goat cheese—US$11

Steamed fillet of red snapper with tomato fondue, grilled eggplant and ginger—US$25

Roasted rack of lamb in herb crust with sautéed artichokes—US$29

les célébrités

This restaurant's name is based on paintings done by celebrities

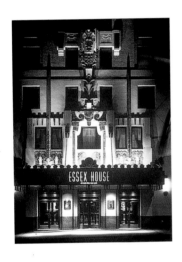

This excellent French restaurant, which some say is the best in New York, thrills patrons with its food and astonishes them with its decor. In the elegantly remodeled Essex House on Manhattan's Central Park South, Les Célébrités is done in the same art deco motif as the hotel. It is the North American flagship property of Nikko Hotels.

The $5 million dining room is modern opulence squared. Its interiors teem with paintings done by such movie stars as James Dean and Phyllis Diller. They are framed and lighted as if they were Picassos but barely hold the spotlight due to the decorative elements elsewhere. Brilliant red draperies, gilt carved woodwork and shiny black marble columns overshadow most of the art.

But the food is not overshadowed. Chef Christian Delouvrier has developed a spectacular cuisine. He says that the hotel does $500,000 a month just in banquet sales, so "I can afford to be extravagant in Les Célébrités." He has a large staff of chefs, all of whom he knew before hiring, for the relatively small dining room.

Delouvrier himself is French and worked in Paris at prestigious restaurants. His first positions in the USA were as executive chef for Air

FROM THE MENU

Burger of fresh duck *foie gras* with Granny Smith apples au jus—US$24

Sautéed and roasted salmon covered with crispy potatoes with a stew of asparagus, wild mushrooms, tomatoes, snow peas, and truffles sauce—US$25

Honey and orange lacquered duck, quenelles of figs, butternut squash and melon—US$34

Well-lighted tables illuminate the luscious appetizers, each presented on different plates. Flowers complement the art deco ambience.

France's Concorde and sous chef at Windows on the World. He was with New York's famed Maurice in the Parker Meridien before he joined Esssex House in 1991.

A little red room with zebra-patterned carpet and soft upholstered chairs serves as the cozy waiting area for Les Célébrités. It, of course, also has entertainers' art.

Seats: 65
Serving: dinner
Covers Sold: 85
Service staff: 14
Kitchen brigade: 22
Check average: US$100
Gross annual sales: US$2 million
Opened: 1991
Affiliations: SRS, AAA
Photography courtesy of Essex House

Hot reds, warm golden tones, shiny black columns and movie stars' artwork all sing out that this is no ordinary restaurant.

les ambassa

Shimmering crystal, polished marble, gold leaf, candlelight and delectable cuisine—the trademarks of Les Ambassadeurs

Perhaps Paris's most palatial hotel, this noble building was once a private mansion belonging to the Counts of Crillon. By 1909 it had become a grandiose hotel with one of the city's most celebrated restaurants. The only hotel privately owned and managed by a French family, it is prestigiously located and magnificently maintained.

Parisian architect Destailleurs undertook the transformation of the ancient structures, maintaining the richness of decoration inherited from its previous owners. He gave the new hotel and its restaurant a level of comfort and luxury deserving of its worldwide reputation. Most recently, designer Sonia Rykiel perfected the interiors so that they function smoothly, are comfortable and eminently luxurious.

Today, guests dining in Les Ambassadeurs with its flawless service and magnificent atmosphere do indeed feel like royalty. Gourmet food has brought countless honors to the restaurant—including two Michelin stars and 17/20 Gault Millau, plus numerous medals won by Chef Christian Constant.

After having worked for world-famous establishments such as L'Ile de France, Ledoyen, Les Anges, and the Ritz Hotel, Constant joined Hôtel de Crillon in 1988 as *chef de cuisine.* In addition to his many medals and certificate of honor, he is a member of the *Societe des Cuisiniers de France et Maitres Cuisiniers de France's* board of directors.

Seats: 60
Serving: breakfast, lunch & dinner
Service staff: 25
Kitchen brigade: 40
Opened: 1981
Affiliations: The Leading Hotels of the World, Relais & Chateaux, Comite Colbert
Photography by Joachim Bonnemaison

above left: In the heart of Paris, in the Place de Concorde, the Hôtel de Crillon is surrounded by fountains, statuary and the Obelisk of Luxor.

90

deurs

Pure white table settings sparkle with candlelight, crystal, silver and red roses.

Couscous de bar. Bar is an ocean fish similar to sea bass, called loup de mer in the Mediterranean.

A beautiful main course, suprême de faisan au foie gras, *is boneless pheasant with goose liver in a mushroom sauce.*

FROM THE MENU

Suggested Prix fixe *dinner FF910 (US$185)*

Crunchy marinated vegetables, lobster from Brittany with acacia honey vinegar

Sautéed fillet of turbot topped with herbs, preserved tomatoes with basil and vinaigrette dressing

Roasted rack of lamb from Pauillac, with moussaka

Seasonal matured cheeses

Iced fresh fennel macaroon, red and black fruits

Salad of lobster from Brittany.

Lavishly inlaid marble, crystal, and gold leaf, all multiplied by glittering mirrors make Les Ambassadeurs truly palatial.

four seasons

Extraordinary food is a trademark of the posh Four Seasons worldwide

Developed for the sophisticated international traveler, or the exacting executive, the Four Seasons restaurant in London is never a bore. If it isn't the exciting cuisine, it's the cheerful, flower-flooded decor or the engaging views through wide windows.

It has retained a Michelin star since 1980 and has collected

FROM THE MENU

Cassoulet terrine wrapped with slivers of Toulouse sausage, cabbage & carrots, flageolet vinaigrette—£3.55 (US$5.60)

Cheese-glazed cannelloni of salmon, eggplant and basil served on Swiss chard, tomato butter sauce and anchovy oil—£9.00 (US$14.25)

Raspberry crunch with almond and pistachio creme—£2.95 (US$4.60)

Light oyster ravioli topped with caviar, cucumber and chervil.

Rosettes from the Automobile Association since 1993—five in 1995.

The à la carte menu at Four Seasons is extensive—ten hors d'oeuvres, seven fish and nine meats are offered. The food is primarily French but much of it is simpler for Chef Jean Christophe Novelli spent several years in the Provence Restaurant in Hampshire, and his approach is altogether creative. Novelli is

also responsible for the "Alternative Cuisine," the low-calorie dishes offered by all Four Seasons hotels.

Proving the difference between "glitz" and glamour, Rosalie Wise, the restaurant's interior designer, has assembled a beautiful room without overdecorating. Prints, arched wall panels, and lighting fixtures provide a Middle Eastern flavor, the chairs introduce a playful pattern, and this is all unified by coral tablecloths and lush plantings.

Seats: 55–65
Serving: lunch & dinner
(4 days/week)
Service staff: 14
Kitchen brigade: 12
Check average: £60 (US$94.50)
Gross annual sales: £1,200,000
(US$1,884,000)
Opened: 1970
Affiliations: The Leading Hotels of the World, Utell
Photography by Jan Baldwin

The restaurant is colorful but serene with its lovely light greens, peach napery and broad windows. Unusual chairs and Oriental lamps are suave touches.

gaddi's

Spaciousness, quietly competent service, simple grandeur, exquisite French food—that is Gaddi's

Gorgeous Gaddi's has the most expensive element in Hong Kong—space. With tables so far apart and ceilings so high, each party enjoys privacy.

FROM THE MENU

Warm lobster salad with a sherry vinegar cream—HK$330 (US$44)

Whole black sea bass baked in pastry for two—HK$700 (US$94)

Roast Guinea fowl with truffle sauce for two—HK$846 (US$110)

Layers of caramelized puff pastry with red fruit and bourbon vanilla ice cream—HK$130 (US$17)

Still giving the aura of a British colony's favorite bailiwick, the legendary Peninsula hotel features eight restaurants but Gaddi's is the most cherished for its French cuisine.

Although Gaddi's has won honors over the past 40 years, its talented new chef will doubtless keep the menus current and creative and will attract even more awards.

Some of Julian Bompard's signature dishes include: bay scallops and prawns served with caviar beurre blanc and a very low-calorie roast Dover sole garnished with Provençale vegetables.

Bompard worked with the famous Louis Outhier in his three-Michelin-star restaurant, L'Oasis on the Côte d'Azur and later at the fabulous Normandie in Bangkok's Oriental. When Bompard worked in Burgundy at the three-Michelin-star restaurant, Lameloise, he learned two cuisines: heavy, traditional Burgundy cuisine and *la cuisine du soleil*— the lighter Provençale influence with vegetables and herbs—just right for the Hong Kong climate.

Seats: 80
Serving: lunch & dinner
Covers sold: 80 (lunch), 80 (dinner)
Service staff: 20
Kitchen brigade: 10
Check Average: HK$350 (US$47) lunch; HK$725 (US$93.75) dinner
Market: hotel guests, local residents both Chinese and Westerners
Opened: 1953
Affiliations: The Leading Hotels of the World, Preferred Hotels & Resorts Worldwide
Photography by Lawrence Yu

A Christmas dinner party at Gaddi's brings forth magical, glittering table decorations.

le chantecler

A glowing, 80-year patina on its priceless wall panels is one of many treasures guests admire

Located in the legendary Hôtel Negresco (built in the belle époque, 1913) on the Côte d'Azur, Le Chantecler has been delighting guests with its museum-quality furnishings and fine cuisine for decades.

The lavish decor is characterized by certified works of art including: Regency wood paneling made in 1751 from the Chateau de Chaintre (near Macon); a rare Aubusson wall tapestry; and a painting by Nattier depicting the Duchess of Orleans, the daughter of Louis XV. On one wall hangs an Aubusson tapestry with a very rare pattern of bouquets of flowers in a Medicean vase.

The Negresco is a rare jewel on the famous Promenade des Anglais in Nice, built in 1913 by architect Edouard Niermans.

Wall coverings and draperies are of pure silk while the carpet is a classic *savonnier-* style typical of the Regency period. Interiors were designed by Madame Augier, the owner. (She and her husband bought the hotel in 1957 after it had been used as a hospital during World War II.)

The inspired cuisine at Le Chantecler is the creation of Chef Dominique Le Stanc, one of France's newer two-Michelin-star chefs. Celebrated today for his cuisine Provençale, Le Stanc's most memorable training was under the famed Allen Senderens of the three-star L'Archestrate in Paris.

As Le Chantecler is on the sea, Le Stanc's menu is filled with seafood; there is even a tasting-menu of all fish. A bounty of fresh local produce and wines of Provence make an extraordinary menu.

Seats: 80
Serving: lunch & dinner
Covers sold: 110 (without breakfast)
Service staff: 16
Kitchen brigade: 22
Check average: FF600 (US$125)
Opened: 1913, remodeled 1967
Affiliations: The Leading Hotels of the World
Photography courtesy of Hôtel Negresco

Graceful period chairs with thick red velvet, colorful savonnier-style carpet and a portrait of the Duchess of Orleans all dignify this gracious room.

Decorated in Regency style by the owner, Madame Augier, Chantecler is magnificent with its sparkling chandeliers and glorious antique wood paneling, vintage 1751.

The only room of the Negresco which has not changed in design since 1913, Le Relais bar is in a pre-1900 English style.

The Salon Regence is connected to the main restaurant by a large doorway. Its walls are white and gold enhanced by engraved leather panels from 1700.

Restaurant
Chantecler

Nice

FROM THE MENU

Open ravioli with asparagus tips, langoustines
and artichokes—FF240 (US$49)

Roast fillet of *daurade* (Mediterranean fish) anise-flavored,
served with asparagus, tomatoes and chervil—FF209 (US$43)

Roast pigeon with cumin, garnished with young potatoes
and red onions—FF195 (US$40)

(Service and tax included)

THE connaught grillroom

Classic French and traditional English cuisine in a refined, very British oasis

A classic building of the late-nineteenth century in London's stylish Mayfair, The Connaught does not pretend to be glamorous but is comfortable and courtly.

One of the most noticed plats du jour on The Connaught's menu is Sole Jubilee, starred as the dish "created for Her Majesty The Queen Elizabeth II Silver Jubilee, 1977." This private place with its calm and serious atmosphere is certainly fitting for royalty.

The Connaught Grillroom was built at a time when the best hotels resembled distinguished English country houses. They recreated an atmosphere that enabled their guests to feel at home in London. The Connaught restaurants are comfortable and home-like for the aristocracy but not fashionable or pretentious.

The tranquil mood owes much to the staff whose care and concern is in accord with the unwritten traditions of English hospitality: warmth of manner, a certain formality and constant attention to detail.

The chef of The Connaught for 22 years, Michel Bourdin, *Maître de Cuisinier de France* is comfortable with dishes ranging from the most complex haute cuisine to classic English specialties. On the dinner menu, printed small in a corner, "Regular Luncheon Dishes"—one for each day of the week—include such old favorites as steak, kidney and mushroom pie.

Seats: 75 (restaurant), 35 (grillroom)
Serving: lunch & dinner
Opened: 1897
Affiliations: Member of Savoy Group, The Leading Hotels of the World
Photography courtesy of The Connaught

Intimate and mahogany-paneled, The Connaught Grillroom prides itself on unobtrusive service and gastronomic excellence.

FROM THE MENU

À la Carte

Kipper Paté—£7.40 (US$11.30)

Coquilles St. Jacques Thermidor or your choice—£28 (US$43.20)

Filet of Beef *en Croute* with light *Strasbourgeoise*—sauerkraut, *foie gras* and salt pork for two—£82 (US$125)

Vegetables in season—£3.70 (US$5.65)

Sherry trifle "Wally Ladd"—£5.75 (US$8.80)

al rubayyat restaurant

A most extraordinary dining adventure takes place within view of the Great Pyramids

Secluded inside the spectacular Mena House Oberoi, an ornate Arabesque hotel, Al Rubayyat serves international dignitaries and leisure travelers the very finest cuisine in Cairo. Even the restaurant address, Pyramids Road Giza, reflects the rare and exotic experience that awaits.

The magnificently proportioned room, enhanced by ogee arches, mushrabia screens and antique Islamic lamps was designed by Eng. Amr al Alfy of the Falcon Company.

To Executive Chef George Khan cooking comes naturally, for his family has been in that profession for generations. Khan learned the art of continental cuisine under various chefs in Europe, then worked in India, the Middle East, London and Geneva.

Though his menus are fairly traditional, with a French flair, he creates

Opposite: Vast and mysterious, Al Rubayyat is a Moroccan design glamorized with Arabesque motifs and immense arches. Starry lighting sparks the shadowy mood.

unusual appetizers such as: escargot in red wine sauce with chopped onions, garlic butter, shrimp and mushrooms; and veal sweetbreads, brain and artichokes in a tarragon sauce, served in puff pastry.

Al Rubayyat is the most alluring of the four dining areas in the beautiful Mena House. This legendary hotel began as a royal lodge, was expanded by 1869 when the Suez Canal opened and today is still serving royalty.

Seats: 250
Serving: lunch & dinner
Service staff: 18
Kitchen brigade: 12
Opened: 1976
Affiliations: Oberoi Hotels International
Photography by Aymen Taher

FROM THE MENU

Homemade duckling terrine with green peppercorn—£E24.60 (US$7.25)

Medallions of veal with asparagus and shrimps, glazed with béarnaise sauce—£E59.50 (US$17.50)

Fillet of red mullet panfried, served with diced shrimp, green peppercorn, capers and tomato concassé—£E44 (US$13)

La Charlotte Royal freshly prepared with orange sauce—£E13.60 (US$4)

Specialties of Al Rubayyat are (top) colorful plating of medallions of veal with asparagus and shrimps, glazed with béarnaise sauce and (above) duckling terrine with green peppercorn.

The giant ogee arch that characterizes Al Rubayyat provides a very grand entrance to this magnificent restaurant.

In keeping with the classic continental and French cuisine, a traditional table setting is used in the theatrical restaurant.

107

les saisons

"Just beautiful!" say guests as they enter this glowing restaurant with its residential style

The lighthearted and lovely Les Saisons may have food with a French accent but its atmosphere most certainly has universal appeal. Its soft, rich look is in vivid contrast with the nine sleek Japanese restaurants in the Imperial Hotel.

The hotel's president/general manager Ichiro Inumaru attended Cornell's famed Hotel School in Ithaca, New York. And he is continually fraternizing with famous hoteliers worldwide, thus he knows what international travelers desire when dining in a fine Tokyo hotel.

A large restaurant with two distinct styles of decor, guests can choose between the casual conservatory section or the more formal stately "living room" areas.

The cuisine is primarily French but is not complicated or esoteric. Dishes are familiar and popular, not selected to appeal only to sophisticated gourmets. In addition, many of the main courses are offered in smaller portions, and many are available in low calorie versions.

The marvelously qualified chef, Hideki Kobayashi, has toured Europe visiting many of the great kitchens. He became *chef de cuisine* of

Like a sunroom in a private home, this parlor of Les Saisons gives a warmth that guests savor.

the Imperial in 1991, but still he had another year and a half training in restaurants such as those in Hotel Richemond and the Royal Club Evian.

Seats: 151
Serving: breakfast, lunch & dinner
Covers sold: 100 (breakfast), 80 (lunch), 90 (dinner)
Service staff: 53
Kitchen brigade: 22
Gross annual sales: US$7,335,360
Opened: 1983
Market: 57.1% local and tourists (76% of whom are Japanese)
Affiliations: The Leading Hotels of the World, SRS, Preferred Hotels & Resorts Worldwide, UTELL, Concorde Hotels
Photography courtesy of Imperial Hotel Co., Ltd.

No expense is spared on flowers and greenery at the Imperial Hotel.

In the more formal section, rich tapestries and damask, carpeting, and soft lighting create elegance.

The contrast of the exquisite tenor of the lower level dining room with the casual wicker and tile sun parlor provides exciting variety in Les Saisons.

FROM THE MENU

Sea urchin soufflé, Les Saisons style—¥3,250 (US$32)

Broiled lobster, fennel flavored—¥5,587 (US$55)

Panfried loin of veal with cured orange
& vegetables—¥5,384 (US$53)

Beefsteak Chaliapin, an Imperial Hotel
original—¥5,587 (US$55)

restaurant daniel

Wizard chef Daniel Boulud attracts New Yorkers

Archways allow patrons to see activity in the dining room en route to the intimate bar; interiors designed by Mara Palmer.

Restaurant Daniel is adjacent to the charming Surrey Hotel that recalls another era with molded ceilings, beveled glass mirrors and antique accents. In contrast, the restaurant has cheerful, guileless interiors, with a warmth that is immediately apparent from such touches as flower boxes nestled under arches. The room is comfortable and conducive to focusing on food.

Chef Daniel brought worldwide fame to Le Cirque for the six years he was its chef. When he opened his own place in 1993, within a year, honors were heaped upon his restaurant. It was named number one in the United States and nine in the world by Patricia Wells, food editor of *The International Herald Tribune.* It also was awarded four stars by the *Mobil Guide* and *The New York Times.*

Named Best Chef in America by the James Beard Foundation, Boulud was brought up on his family's farm in Lyons where he came to appreciate fresh produce and his grandmother's simple cooking. In France he worked under great chefs including Michael Guerard, Roger Vergé and Georges Blanc. Chef Boulud is currently a columnist for *Elle Decor Magazine* and is author of *Cooking with Daniel Boulud.*

Ms. Wells describes his ability aptly, "He offers food with a homespun quality sparked with glimmers of upscale classic French....and at moments he displays flashes of simple brilliance, with a celery coulis embellishing a curried tuna tartar."

Seats: 85
Serving: lunch (Tuesday–Friday), dinner (Monday–Saturday)
Service staff: 32
Kitchen brigade: 30
Check average: US$70 dinner
Opened: 1993
Affiliations: Manhattan East Suite Hotels
Photography courtesy of The Surrey Hotel

Restaurant Daniel's warm and welcoming dining room exudes a casual chic ambiance highlighted by an abundance of flowers and contemporary art.

FROM THE MENU

Chilled five spring pea soup with bacon and a rosemary-infused cream—US$12

Oregon morels stuffed with squab and *foie gras*—US$23

Atlantic sea bass in a crisp potato shell with red wine sauce—US$34

Gratin of tarragon infused bittersweet chocolate—US$33

sea grill
j. le divellec

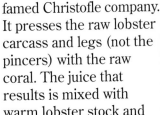

This trim, unpretentious restaurant wins awards for its superior seafood served amid original art

Homard à la Presse

RESTAURANT
Sea Grill

No 000053

Furnished with Scandinavian simplicity and quality, Sea Grill has impressive glass wall murals of Norway's fjords and shell sculptures that seem to float. Jacques Le Divellec, the owner and chef of Le Divellec in Paris is known internationally for his style of fish cookery.

In addition to training under Le Divellec in Paris, Yves Mattagne, the youngest *maître de cuisine* in Belgium, worked in the Hilton Internationals in Brussels and Gatwick, England. His culinary competence has not been overlooked as the Sea Grill has received one

There are three lobster presses extant today—one at the inventor's restaurant, one in the Christofle museum, and one at the Sea Grill.

star from the Michelin Guide, 16/20 from Gault Millau plus 2 toques rouge, and 92/100 from Le Grand Guide Henry Lemaire.

The high level of service at the Sea Grill is due to Marc Meremans, the manager who rose from assistant maître d' in 1991 to his present position. In 1993 he won the Maître d'Hotel Oscar from *Le Club des Gastronomes.*

A dramatic tableside preparation is carried out with the Lobster Press, invented by J. Le Divellec in 1991, and made by the

Simplicity and quality in an environment that recalls the sea personifies the Sea Grill at the Radisson SAS Royal Hotel.

famed Christofle company. It presses the raw lobster carcass and legs (not the pincers) with the raw coral. The juice that results is mixed with warm lobster stock and whipped cream which is poured over the panfried lobster meat.

Seats: 80
Serving: lunch & dinner
Covers sold: 110 (daily)
Service staff: 11
Kitchen brigade: 10
Check average: BF 2,950 (US$100)
Market: 10% hotel guests, 90% local
Opened: 1990
Affiliations: Radisson SAS Hotels Worldwide
Photography courtesy of Radisson SAS Royal Hotel

Left and above: Murals of the Norway fjords, and floating shells on a Lucite structure adorn the walls. Interiors were designed by Belgian Nicolas Lecompte.

FROM THE MENU

Whole sea bass roasted and flamed with thyme cream and shallots—BF887 (US$30)

Dublin Bay prawns steamed in a basket with basil light Biscayenne sauce in a crispy envelope—BF592 (US$35)

Pressed Brittany lobster prepared at table—BF592 (US$20) per 100 grams

le gavroche

This is London's first claim to French culinary fame

L e Gavroche has been the most honored French restaurant in London since 1967 when it was opened in relatively small quarters by Albert and Michel Roux. By 1981 it moved to prestigious Mayfair where it is now on the ground floor of a luxurious 52-suite hotel—Forty-seven Park Street.

Le Gavroche with its rich reds, padded seating, and residential touches is intimate, but patrons come for the culinary experience, not a luxuriant setting.

Michel A. Roux, son of Albert Roux, is now the chef of Le Gavroche, having studied in Europe and trained with his father before taking over. Today Albert still supervises, and brother Michel has other engrossments including Waterside Inn, a popular place in Berkshire.

Two Michelin stars and three Egon Ronay stars are among the kudos earned by young Michel. He still keeps his fathers favorites on the menu but has written a splendid menu himself. He does somewhat lighter, basically French cooking.

About 40 cheeses are offered—all French except Stilton and Parmesan—along with six kinds of bread. In addition, nine irresistible desserts are on the menu. But true connoisseurs also focus on the incredible wines collected by Le Gavroche. The wine list has 818 different bins plus 20 ports, and a convenient listing of those that are stocked in half bottles.

Gelée aux oranges et framboise au whiskey. The raspberries peek through the aspic.

Seats: 60
Serving: lunch & dinner
Covers sold: 60 (lunch),
120 (dinner)
Serving staff: 35
Kitchen brigade: 35
Check average: £80 (US$125.60)
Opened: 1967
Affiliations: Relais Gourmand,
Traditions & Qualite,
Maitre Cuisines de France
Photography by Martin Brigdale

Traditionally furnished and very comfortable, Le Gavroche sets an exquisite table in all white contrasting nicely with the radiant reds of the carpet.

FROM THE MENU

Soufflé Suissesse—£19.80 (US$32)

L'assiette du boucher—£33.80 (US$53)

Omelette Rothschild (soufflé with apricots and Cointreau)—£16.60 (US$26)

(Service and VAT included)

mark's restaurant

Not overly ornate or trendy, Mark's is luxurious but comfortable

Like a lovely living room, Mark's makes guests feel comfortable while being indulged with splendid service and cuisine.

That Mark's Restaurant would be an award winner in every guide book and magazine is no surprise. Given the location, the elegance of the hotel, the nature of General Manager Raymond Bickson and the caliber of the managing company, Rafael Group, it was inevitable that this restaurant would win top recognition from New York's hard-to-please diners and critics.

Bickson and George Rafael, managing director of the group, agreed that Mark's would not just be a dining room for the convenience of the hotel guests, but would be one that could stand alone as a fine restaurant. This is the path that the Rafael Group has taken with all its small luxury hotels.

Rafael wants Mark's to be part of the community, not isolated from it. Bickson urges neighbors in the fine residential area to dine and relax in Mark's. Dress is up to the patrons, and despite the sophisticated decor, it is a casual restaurant.

Chef Philippe Boulot, a young Frenchman with impressive credentials (Four Seasons Clift, London's Four Seasons, L'Archestrate, and Maxims in Paris) contends that no chef should use the hotel as a stage for his own experimentation and ego-building. He should consider the guests' tastes.

Boulot draws on cuisine bourgeoisie which relies on classic French cooking techniques and fresh ingredients. He changes the menus daily, and espouses contemporary American cooking.

Seats: 80
Serving: breakfast, lunch, tea & dinner
Covers sold: 175 (daily)
Service staff: 25
Kitchen brigade: 23
Check average: US$35.90
Gross annual sales: US$1.5 million
Opened: 1990
Affiliations: Rafael Hotels, The Leading Hotels of the World, Small Luxury Hotels of the World, Utell, Prima
Photography courtesy of The Mark

The svelte entry to Mark's (below) contrasts pleasingly with the rich, residential look in the dining room.

FROM THE MENU

Prix fixe Luncheon US$28
Caesar salad with prosciutto and sun-dried tomatoes; Gravlax and dill fritata; Mark's fruit soup,
vanilla, lemon grass

Prix fixe Dinner US$48
Snails in potato crust; Roasted veal chop, brus-
sels sprouts, glazed apple, calvadoes sauce;
Mango mousse with apricot sauce

121

restaurant pétrus

On the 56th floor of Hong Kong's tallest hotel, guests enjoy lofty wining and dining

Breathtaking views of Hong Kong's lively harbor, shining financial district and picturesque Victoria Peak are all cherished from sumptuously decorated Pétrus. The elaborate accessories around the diners are in tune with the brilliant French food, wine and service.

Named after the famous French Chateau Pétrus wines, the restaurant holds the world's largest collection of Pétrus wines. *Wine Spectator* magazine honored Pétrus for its excellent wine lists, from specialty lists that emphasize wines of one country or region to lists that cover the world.

The hotel holds more than 12,000 bottles of wine in controlled temperature cellars, the rarest of which are displayed in glass cases in the restaurant.

The honors Petrus boasts are countless; perhaps the most meaningful recent ones are: "The Best All Around Hong Kong," by *Gourmet* magazine's Fred Ferritti, and "Best French Restaurant" by *Hong Kong Magazine.*

The only three-Michelin-star *chef de cuisine* in Hong Kong is Gerard Cavuscens of Petrus. A Swiss, he had more than 20 years of culinary experience while working in various Michelin-starred restaurants in Switzerland and France, highlighted by six years as *chef de cuisine* at the famed Restaurant Girardet in Crissier.

A richness in Pétrus interiors shines in marble statues, flowers, paintings, and amply sized chairs, all designed by Paul Leese.

Though Cavuscens' cooking is decidedly French, he often creates international delights such as: tagliatelle on a lemon grass cream sauce, with baby squid stuffed with ginger, capsicum and herbs. Currently his kudos are the result of his many, highly creative *foie gras* dishes.

Seats: 88
Serving: lunch & dinner
Serving staff: 19
Kitchen brigade: 14
Check average: HK$975
(US$125)
Opened: 1991
Affiliations: Shangri-La Hotels & Resorts
Photography by Jaime Ardiles-Arce

A spacious room, Petrus contains all manner of glitter and grace. The chandeliers and recessed ceilings provide beauty.

FROM THE MENU

Sautéed slice of gooseliver with sesame and poppy seeds served with a sherry vinegar gravy—HK$180 (US$23)

Sliced gooseliver stuffed with raisins and walnuts in a Gewurztraminer jelly—HK$200 (US$25)

Terrine of gooseliver with a celeriac and apple remoulade—HK$180 (US$23)

Scallop roesti served with a spring salad seasoned with balsamic vinegar dressing—HK$260 (US$33)

Roast rack of lamb with cinnamon and red curry, accompanied by eggplant gratin—HK$280 (US$36)

A fantasyland view with luxurious dining accoutrements, Petrus thrills its patrons with foie gras *dishes and a much praised wine cellar.*

pierrot

This heavenly place is named for Picasso's painting of his son

Pierrot, atop the Mandarin Oriental, has a stunning view of Hong Kong Harbor.

An absolutely first rate, luxurious French restaurant, Pierrot is located on the top floor of the Mandarin Oriental, a hotel whose understated Oriental grandeur is unrivaled. According to one critic, "The quest for perfection at the Mandarin lives on as a legend."

Stepping from the 25th floor into Pierrot, guests enter an impressive penthouse lobby with gold-inlaid, black marble flooring. Two large flower urns flank the entrance to the Harlequin Bar. Inside, Regency striped armchairs and low tables surround a circular marble bar.

The Harlequin Bar and Pierrot have both been refurbished by interior designers Cowperthwaite & Partners who complemented bold plum and midnight blue fabrics with a striking carpet in blue and gold. The wide windows offering scenic views are framed with ornate draperies.

The cuisine at Pierrot is French with a contemporary flair. Dinner is à la carte and luncheon features seasonal foods with fixed prices. Chef Peter Find who early in 1995 joined Pierrot has impressive credentials: he was sous chef of three important German restaurants. He also worked with the renowned Anton Mosimann in London.

The first caviar restaurant in Asia, Petrossian caviar is served alone or in the preparation of appetizers and main courses.

Seats: 65
Serving: lunch & dinner
Maître d': Philippe Bru
Opened: 1979
Affiliations: The Leading Hotels of the World
Photography courtesy of Mandarin Oriental

Salon Cartier, Pierrot's private dining room is well named as all of its tableware, glassware and silver are Cartier designs.

FROM THE MENU

Panfried escallop of goose liver on candied shallot and artichoke compote with olive essence—HK $295 (US$38)

Scrambled farm-fresh eggs with Sevruga caviar—HK $147 (US$19)

Savarin of spaghetti on thin slices of Maine lobster marinated in a roasted turbot and curry vinaigrette—HK $279 (US$36)

Shark's fin in vodka cream with Sevruga pearls—HK $145 (US$19)

Scrambled farm-fresh eggs with Sevruga Caviar.

lespinasse

Unique French-Asian cuisine in a quietly beautiful French restaurant

Part of the wonder of Lespinasse is that it is polished and glowing but looks as if it were still part of that gorgeous old 1904 St. Regis building. The classical proportions of the room are thanks to Graham Design which created receding arches, alcoves and vestibules, then clustered the tables on the perimeter to give a sense of intimacy.

The wood paneling, pilasters and delicate Louis XV and XVI style furniture all create a creamy, light tone, making a proper stage for the abundant flowers throughout the restaurant. The 22-karat gold leaf that outlines the molding and trim in Lespinasse adds to its grandeur.

The restaurant has a separate entrance discreetly located a few yards from the hotel's bronze and glass doors. The dining room itself is tucked away behind the impressive Astor Court.

Providing food to fit all this finery is the skilled Chef Gray Kunz whose remarkable cooking has won Lespinasse the AAA Five Diamond award. Swiss-trained in the kitchens of Europe's great hotels, then a sous chef to the famed Freddy Girardet, Kunz eventually was put in command at Plume in The Regent Hong Kong where he gained respect and love for oriental spices and flavors. Chef Kunz cooks in several languages now. In praise of his oriental bent, many say that his real signature dish is steamed black sea bass served in a bowl with a Thai-inspired kaffir lime-leaf emulsion.

Seats: 85
Serving: breakfast, lunch & dinner
Covers sold: 300 (daily)
Service staff: 39
Kitchen brigade: 34
Opened: 1991
Affiliations: The Luxury Collection, ITT Sheraton
Photography courtesy of The St. Regis

A Waterford crystal chandelier, exquisite silk fabrics and Limoges china custom designed by Tiffany are among the many luxurious accoutrements at Lespinasse.

Lespinasse

FROM THE MENU

Spiced-glazed salmon with bean and sweet corn stew—US$35

Rack of lamb on curried eggplant tart with carrot emulsion—US$3

Herbed risotto and mushroom fricassee—US$22

Warm chocolate tartlet with passion fruit coulis —US$14

THE hassler roof restaurant

Half the skyline of Rome can be seen from this dining room in the sky

The Hassler Roof Restaurant is situated on the sixth floor of the Hassler, revealing a panoramic view of Rome. The hotel occupies one of the highest and broadest sites in the city so that the grandeur of the skyline is easily visible.

The historic Hassler first opened on its present site in 1885. After renovation of the hotel in 1948 the Roof was used as a tea room. In the 1950s the present rooftop restaurant was created, and has been refurbished frequently by designer Hans-Peter Karch.

The Hassler has been managed by the Wirth family for more than 90 years so its care and grooming have been carefully attended to. Present General Manager Roberto Wirth proudly says that

the international elite gather on the Roof to enjoy the traditional, refined Mediterranean cuisine.

Some of the delectable dishes that frequent customers like to order (in addition to those listed "From the Menu") include: sea bass "Caprese" seasoned with basil oil, served with tomatoes and mozzarella; eggplant and zucchini rolls with Buffalo mozzarella and casserole of salmon and zucchini with chervil.

One of the most artistically presented salads is one in which the prawns and rucola are plated as a spiral; it is dressed with botargo vinaigrette.

At the top of the famous Spanish Steps in Rome to the right of Trinity Mount Church is the Hotel Hassler.

Occupying one of the highest and broadest sites in Rome, Hassler reveals a panoramic view of the city from the sixth floor.

The decor is simple and handsome, not competing with the delectable cuisine nor the breathtaking vistas.

Desserts are displayed prominently in the center of the restaurant, mingled with flower bouquets.

For banquets and other special events, the Hassler will prepare personalized menus for parties of up to 90 people. An enforced dress code in the evenings requires that gentlemen wear coats and ties. During Sunday brunch the Roof comes alive with piano music.

Seats: 90
Serving: breakfast, lunch, dinner & Sunday brunch
Service staff: 19
Kitchen brigade: 13
Opened: 1944
Affiliations: The Leading Hotels of the World
Photography courtesy of Hotel Hassler

A lovely spot in which to enjoy Hassler's fine wines—in the afternoon looking at the twin domes of Trinity.

The Hassler Roof Restaurant

FROM THE MENU

Zucchini flowers filled with mousse
of smoked salmon—L34,500 (US$23)

Fish filled ravioli in a sauce of lobster
and light tomato—L33,000 (US$22)

Medallions of veal filet flavored with
limoncello liqueur—L54,000 (US$36)

(Service and tax included)

verandah

Romantic Lake Como, an ancient villa, and superb Italian cuisine!

Since 1961, Verandah has been a grand dining destination for tourists and regulars who return each summer to enjoy Chef Luciano Parolari's irresistible Italian food. He changes the menu daily, creating a dozen specials to excite the adventurous diners, and happily provides classics for his conservative guests.

Service at Verandah, as in the whole resort, is wonderfully attentive for the staff outnumbers the guests. Chef Parolari has supervised the Villa's kitchens for 20 years and has traveled the world teaching his cooking techniques. He has written two cookbooks, and his most recent honor was to be guest chef at the United Nations Delegates Dining Room when it had an Italian Food & Wine Festival.

Within view of the Swiss Alps, not far from Milan, Villa d'Este is located in a wooded park midst gardens and fountains, overlooking the blue-green waters of Lake Como. The Villa was built in 1568 as a summer residence for Cardinal Tolomeo Gallio and remained in the Gallio family for two centuries.

Then, for many years, aristocrats of Europe lived in the Villa. In 1815 it was owned by the Princess of Wales, later the wife of King George IV of England. Finally, in 1873 a company of wealthy Milanese transformed it into a luxury hotel. The hotel was totally renovated recently without disturbing the original Neoclassical Renaissance facades and the buildings' old world charm.

Seats: 200
Serving: breakfast, lunch & dinner
Covers: 310
Service staff: 31
Kitchen brigade: 36
Check average: L80,000 (US$50)
Affiliations: The Leading Hotels of the World
Photography by Antonio Vasconi

Verandah restaurant overlooks gorgeous gardens and a cardinal's ancient villa

A sybaritic experience: dining at Verandah enjoying the glorious grounds, impeccable service, and epicurean delights from the Italian Chef Luciano Parolari.

FROM THE MENU

Antipasto Villa d'Este, lobster, *foie gras,* salmon—L49,500
(US$31)

Turbot with shrimp and olives—L42,000 (US$26)
Veal liver Venetian style with polenta croutons—L38,000
(US$24)

Risotto with scampi and lemon—L26,000 (US$16.50)

Tagliolini with mussels and vegetables—L26,000 (US$16.50)

masa's

Red velvet sets the tone for this intimate, almost mysterious hideaway

The full-service bar at Masa's is intimate and romantic.

"**S**eductive and elusive" seems to describe Masa's. It is a hugely popular French restaurant that is difficult to book.

Despite the glamour, it is the food that lures guests. Prepared by award-winning Executive Chef Julian Serrano, the cuisine is based on creativity and unusual ingredients—New Zealand venison, roast breast of pheasant with morels and pears, and warm lobster salad with crispy leeks and truffles vinaigrette. These wondrous dishes are part of the tasting menu, a culinary adventure for US$75. And to crown any meal at Masa's, diners can enjoy a dessert tasting platter.

Serrano, a native of Madrid, started at Masa's in 1984 and was personally trained by the restaurant's founding chef, Masa Kobayashi. "Masa gave my life to me," says Serrano who finally realized he too could be creative and make beautiful things. *San Francisco Magazine* voted Serrano Chef of the Year 1994, and the Napa Valley Wine Auction of 1995 chose him as their chef.

It takes an active and focused maître d' to smoothly manage a busy restaurant. Since 1986 James Soule has been responsible for the fine service and for working with the knowledgeable sommelier Burke Owens.

Seats: 65
Serving: dinner (Tuesday–Saturday, 6:30-9:30)
Check average: US$100 per person including beverages
Service staff: 15
Kitchen brigade: 15
Opened: 1983
Affiliations: Kimpton Hotel & Restaurant Group
Photography by David Wakely

FROM THE MENU

Prix fixe dinner US$68

Boudin of fresh lobster, shrimp and scallops with two sauces

Foie gras sauté with Madeira truffle sauce

Lamb noisettes with green peppercorns, sauce zinfandel

Dark chocolate and Cointreau terrine with Tahitian vanilla sherbet

Right: Reds and burgundies with pin-point lighting on each table give a regal ambience to the dining room.

goya

THE HOTEL RITZ MADRID

Colorful Goya offers a hearty Spanish menu that will intrigue gourmets

Like so many of the grand old buildings in Madrid, The Hotel Ritz, its garden and its restaurant are beautiful and timeless. Warm, refined and, admittedly, exclusive, no other Madrid hotel possesses so much history and yet no other is so modern.

Goya reveals its spirit easily as it opens into the lobby, attracting guests. With all its bright colors, lovely chandeliers and marble columns, diners find it a pleasurable place to sample the Spanish cuisine. Its name is apt indeed for the restaurant faces the great Prado across the street where so many of Goya's great paintings are on exhibit.

A Forte Exclusive Hotel, it has been renovated and yet still keeps its desirable patina from 1910. The Food & Beverage Manager Manuela Turiño says, "Our ultimate aim is quality and efficiency, bringing together the best of classical catering with an understanding of the new demands of our guests."

The chefs, Ramón Dimanuel and Javier Aldea have worked in the hotel since 1980 having gained wide experience by traveling and working in other hotels in the Forte chain.

Seats: 100
Serving: breakfast, lunch & dinner
Service staff: 26
Kitchen brigade: 22
Market: 50% hotel guests; 50% local
Opened: 1910
Affiliations: Forte Hotels, The Leading Hotels of the World, Utell
Photography courtesy of The Hotel Ritz, Madrid

Sunday brunch is cheerful with an endless assortment of foods — Western breakfasts, Spanish specialties, varied meats, fruits, cheeses and pastries.

Intricately created tapestries and carpets combine with classical architecture—arched windows, mirrored doors—to make a bright, lively atmosphere.

FROM THE MENU

6,900 Pesetas (US$60) for any of the following:

Toledian lentils stew, grilled lamb

Madrilenian "Cocido" (bacon, meat & chick-pea casserole)

Codfish with chick-pea soup

Madrilenian "Cocido," Tripe Madrilenian style

Fabida Asturiana (rich butter bean and pork stew)

Zarzuela of fish & seafood

THE formal dining room

Hawaii has countless luxurious paradises but this "mountain" lodge and dining room are extraordinary

Rare indeed to be dining in Hawaii surrounded by pines, high altitude and cool climate, but that is the incredible environment found at The Lodge at Koele. The Formal Dining Room seems to have been transported right out of a country gentleman's estate.

The location in Lanai's central country highlands affects the whole dining enterprise. Foods are heavier with country cooking; the decor is Northern, dark and rich, with a fireplace to warm guests. They are hungry from their strenuous outdoor mountain activities. Salads are out, cassoulet is in. Even the dress code is different—jacket and tie are required and no one objects.

Though the location is remote, the cuisine is sheer sophistication. Says Chef Edwin Gotto, "I often prepare ragout specials, from braised vegetables to lamb-shanks with soft herbed polenta. I also like earthy ingredients such as artichokes, forest mushrooms and fava beans."

"I'm fortunate to be cooking on an island

An inviting decor with fireplace, lush plants and colorful service plates creates warmth and charm. Photo by Arnold Savrann.

A dessert to tantalize and delight patrons is red pear Napoleon with anise sauce. Note the dancing girl atop. Photo by Jeffrey Asher.

Pan-roasted duck with lemon spaetzle and sun-dried cranberry jus. Photo by Jeffrey Asher.

Seared opa with riso pasta and lemon butter sauce. Photo by Jeffrey Asher.

A spectacular presentation is given to the roasted Lanai venison loin with mashed and fried sweet potatoes, one of the chef's specialties. Photo by Jeffrey Asher.

FROM THE MENU

Wild game sausage with stewed leeks and cabbage, sun-dried cherry mustard sauce—US$11

Japanese eggplant terrine, toasted goat cheese and crushed plum tomatoes—US$9.25

Roast Lanai venison loin with mashed and fried sweet potatoes—US$35

Pan-roasted duck with lemon spaetzle and sun-dried cranberry jus—US$28.50

The dining interior has singular elements: giant candlesticks, graceful light fixtures, and chairs with pineapples carved in the backs. Photo by Arnold Savrann.

where I'm able to obtain quality ingredients," continues Gotto, "I work with local farmers for our special produce, use fish from local waters and venison from nearby forests." But sparks of elegance are introduced in Gotto's menu with *foie gras* and chanterelles.

Gotto's experience is varied. He worked in restaurants in Oahu, then in 1983 joined the Halekulani's famed La Mer, then Nikko Hotel and Park Hyatt in San Francisco. In 1992 he came to The Lodge at Koele, a place he and everyone else loves.

Seats: 64
Serving: dinner
Covers sold: 90
Service staff: 15
Kitchen brigade: 30
Check average:
US$40 without beverages
Gross annual sales: $1.2 million
Opened: 1990
Affiliations: Preferred Hotels & Resorts Worldwide, Select Hotels & Resorts International
Photography by Jeffrey Asher, Arnold Savrann

THE grill room

The best of British cooking, midst an unexpected baronial Spanish-style interior

Few restaurants can boast of having the same decor and menu for 65 years yet still be highly popular. The Dorchester's Grill Room is one of these rare dining retreats.

Traditional British dishes may be the main thrust of the menu but the red velvet, filigreed brass, tapestries and tasseled window treatments spell rich, old Spain. This historic hotel was completely renovated in 1989–90. The Grill Room was renewed with perhaps even more embellishment.

Willie Eisener, an intensively trained Swiss culinarian, was appointed executive chef of The Dorchester's kitchens in 1988. He had been invited two years before to be sous chef to the celebrated Anton Mosimann who built the hotel's matchless culinary reputation.

Eisener's approach to cooking is based on three principles: the value of tradition; experience; and the need for good nutrition

The elevators outside the Grill Room repeat the ornate brass filigree of the dining areas.

with one constant and essential ingredient—freshness.

Seats: 81
Serving: breakfast, lunch & dinner
Covers sold: 90-100 (breakfast), 40-70 (lunch), 50-90 (dinner)
Service staff: 30
Kitchen brigade: 28
Check average: £26.50 (US$44.50) lunch & dinner
Affiliations: The Leading Hotels of the World, Utell
Photography by Richard Greenly

FROM THE MENU

Morecambe Bay potted shrimp—£8.50 (US$13.50)

Roast Angus beef with Yorkshire pudding and roast potatoes—£19.50 (US$31)

Braised oxtail with vegetables—£22.50 (US$35.50)

Set luncheon menu for £24.50 (US$40) changes daily, includes such English specialties as:
Boiled silverside with carrots, onions and dumplings

Whole roast saddle of lamb with thyme

Steak and kidney pudding

The intricate gilt ceiling, tapestry and elaborately patterned carpet make this a majestic room.

145

le restaurant

Australia proves that high-rise dining can indeed include haute cuisine

Spectacular views east and north across the city parallel the splendor of the grand dining experience synonymous with Le Restaurant.

High on the Melbourne skyline, 35 floors up in the sleek Regent Hotel, this urbane dining room, Le Restaurant, is a place for special occasions. Tourists, business executives, locals and hotel guests find it an exciting venue for celebrations. It first opened in 1982, immediately after the lavish skyscraper hotel became The Regent (now a part of the Regent-Four Seasons group).

That Le Restaurant is only open for dinner on Tuesdays through Saturdays makes its US$2 million annual sales figures the more remarkable. But the future looks even brighter because the new executive chef, Austrian-born and trained Wolfgang von Wieser, who took over in January 1995, has produced highly imaginative menus that critics praise. He prefers a light touch with few butter and cream sauces.

Von Wieser most recently was with the Four Seasons Hotel in Vancouver and it was there that he developed his "Pacific Rim Cuisine"—combining Asian, Californian and South Pacific foods.

The menu degustation is six courses of unique creations that Melbourne's gourmets appreciate. From pheasant and hare terrine to Stilton sourdough bread pudding, it's full of surprises.

Keeping Le Restaurant prosperous while pleasing customers, Manager

Evening provides a glittering vista for diners, especially those lucky enough to have window seats. The interiors were designed by Robert Lym of Pei, Cobb, Freed and Partners, New York.

Jack Vanderhelm gives the best service, but "Alas, everyone wants a window seat!"

Seats: 100
Serving: dinner (Tuesdays–Saturdays)
Covers sold: 60–70 weekdays, 100 (Fridays & Saturdays)
Service staff: 13
Kitchen brigade: 9
Gross annual sales: US$2 million
Check average: US$60 without beverages
Market: 39% hotel guests
Photography by Perspective Images

146

FROM THE MENU

Seared tenderloin of South Australian grain-fed beef with Thai-inspired *beurre blanc*—A$33.40 (US$25)

Medallions of Gippsland lamb loin with an eggplant confit, capsicum baronet and potato puree—A$30.70 (US$23)

Mixed grill of Tasmanian salmon with saffron fried risotto—A$34 (US$25)

Trio of Oscietre caviar and buckwheat blinis is a stylish starter at Le Restaurant. Plate presentations are stunning.

Red Capsicum Soup (a medley of chili peppers) is one of von Wieser's popular items, especially during the winters.

Left: Le Restaurant's interior is designed to let the boundless view prevail.

The focal spot of Le Restaurant's windowless space is a trompe l'oeil of a Greco-Roman facade and French garden.

eden-roc

This romantic restaurant thrills guests with spectacular water views and exquisite French cuisine

On the luxuriant grounds of the grand Hôtel du Cap, at the end of the little peninsula of Cap d'Antibes, France, Eden-Roc is the dining choice of international business people, royalty, heads of state and Hollywood celebrities. Not only does the blue Mediterranean surround the hotel, but verdant pine forests and lush gardens add to the grandeur.

The panorama of this central Riviera spot extends along the rocky coast and includes the Iles de Lerins and beyond the Esterel skyline. Isolated, yet halfway between Nice and Cannes, this bit of Eden is 30 minutes from the Nice airport and accessible by yacht from the entire Côte d'Azur.

Luxurious Eden-Roc is quite separate from the aristocratic Hôtel du Cap, which was built in 1870. To reach the restaurant and pool, perched on the edge of the sea, guests walk through lovely gardens. Jean Claude Irondelle, managing director and Mme Irondelle have upgraded and beautified Eden-Roc's interiors since the new seaside complex was added in 1929.

One of the foremost hoteliers of Europe, Irondelle keeps the 110-room hotel and 200-seat restaurant busy and profitable seven months a year, without belonging to any marketing group. He believes in word-of-mouth advertising and depends on repeat customers, many of whom

On the rocky coast, where twinkling lights from the Côte d'Azur's city of Nice enhance the vistas, lies the Eden-Roc restaurant and terrace.

Eden-Roc restaurant faces the glorious Mediterranean with its spectacular views. Formally set tables on bright white cloths contrast with the rich, dark carpeting.

request their favorite tables, or their special rooms.

Arnaud Poette is Eden-Roc's chef. Though only 35 he has been with Eden-Roc since 1983, having trained at the Ecole Hoteliére of Soisson.

Seats: 100–200 (depending on weather)
Serving: breakfast, lunch & dinner
Average check: US$110 per person per day for hotel guests
Covers sold: 200 (dinner)
Serving staff: 30
Kitchen brigade: 20
Photography by Mr. Bompuis

Loup de mer (sea bass) with basil and fennel mousseline—FF295 (US$60)

Grilled duckling breast with honey & sesame seeds; spinach, celery ravioli —FF210 (US$45)

Wild strawberries on biscuits and puree of citrus fruits—FF52 (US$18)

The spacious, stylish Eden Roc interiors were created by the managing director of Hôtel du Cap, Jean Claude Irondelle, and his wife. The room comes alive with the abundant flowers, supervised by Mme Irondelle.

On Eden Roc's incredible buffet, a harnessed lobster pulls a chariot and acts as a serving plate for fish mousse.

To dramatize their delectable desserts, Chef Poette and his pastry chef created a masterfully sculptured bird.

153

directory

AL RUBAYYAT RETAURANT
The Mena House Oberoi Hotel & Casino
Pyramids Rd., Giza
Cairo, Egypt
Tel: 3833222/3833444
Fax: 3837777

Executive Chef: George Khan

Architecture/Restaurant Design: Eng. Amr al Alfy,
Falcon Company

THE BLACK FOREST
Brenner's Park-Hotel & Spa
Schillerstraße 6
Baden-Baden 76530
Germany
Tel: (7221) 90 00
Fax: (7221) 38772

Chef: Albert Kellner
Maître d': René Gonnard
Manager: Richard Schmitz

Architecture: Professor Caesar F. Pinnau,
Architekten Michael von Heppe

CAFE PIERRE
The Pierrre
Fifth Avenue @ 61st Street
New York, NY 10021
Tel: (212) 940-8185
Fax: (212) 750-0541

Executive Chef: Franz Klampfer
Chef: Bertrand Vernejoul
Manager: Charlotte Akoto

THE CAUSERIE
Claridge's
Brook Street, Mayfair
London, England W1A 2JQ
Tel: (0171) 629-8860
Fax: (0171) 499-2210

Chef: Marjan Lesnik
Manager: Peter Mand

CLUB DEL DOGE
Gritti Palace Hotel
Campo Santa Maria del Giglio, 2467- San Marco
Venice, Italy 30124
Tel: 0039-41-794611
Fax: 0039-41-5200942

Chef: Celestino Giacomello
Maître d': Davide Spader

THE CONNAUGHT GRILLROOM
The Connaught
Carlos Place, Mayfair
London, England W1Y 6AL
Tel: (44) 171-499-7070
Fax: (44) 171-495-3262

Chef de Cuisine: Michel Bourdin
Managing Director/General Manager: Paolo Zago

Architecture: Isaacs and Florence

THE CONSERVATORY
The Lanesborough
Hyde Park Corner
London, England SW1X 7TA
Tel: (0171) 259-5599
Fax: (0171) 259-5606

Executive Chef: Paul Gayler
Manager: Geoffrey Gelardi

Architecture: William Wilkins
Restaurant Design: Ezra Attia Associates

THE DINING ROOM
The Ritz-Carlton, Buckhead
3434 Peachtree Road, NE
Atlanta, Georgia 30326
Tel: (404) 237-2700

Chef: Guenter Seeger
Maître d'/Manager: Peter Krehan
Master Sommelier: Michael McNeill

Architecture: Smallwood, Reynolds, Stewart & Stewart
Restaurant Design: Frank Nicholson, Inc.

EDEN-ROC
Hotel du Cap
Boulevard Kennedy, B.P.29 06601 Antibes
France
Tel: (93) 61-39-01
Fax: (93) 67-76-04

Chef: Arnaud Poette
Maître d': Giancarlo Colombo
Managing Director: Jean-Claude Irondelle

Architecture: Jacques Dupay

THE FORMAL DINING ROOM
The Lodge at Koele
P.O. Box 310
Lana'i City, HI 96763
Tel: (808) 565-7300
Fax: (808) 565-4561

Executive Chef: Edwin Goto

Architecture: Arnold Savrann,
Dole Food Company, Inc.
Restaurant Design: Joszi Meskan & Associates
Interior Architecture & Design

FOUR SEASONS
Four Seasons Hotel (London)
Hamilton Place, Park Lane
London W1A 1Az
Tel: (44) 171-499-0888
Fax: (44) 71-493-1895

Chef de Cuisine: Jean Christophe Novelli
Maître d': Vinicio Paolini

Architecture: Michael Rosenauer
Restaurant Design: Rosalie Wise, Rosalie Wise Design

GADDI'S
The Peninsula
Salisbury Road, Tsimshatsui
Kowloon, Hong Kong
Tel: (852) 2366-6251
Fax: (852) 2315-3140

Chef: Julien Bompard
Maître d': Rolf Heiniger

Restaurant Design: David Beer,
Brennan Beer Gorman Monk/Interiors

GOYA
The Hotel Ritz
Plaza de la Lealtad, 5
Madrid, Spain 28014
Tel: (91) 521-28-57
Fax: (91) 532-87-76

Chefs: Ramón Dimanuel, Javier Aldea
Maître d': Luis Méndez
Manager: Manuela Turiño

THE GRILL ROOM
The Dorchester
Park Lane
London, England WIA 2HJ
Tel: (0171) 629-8888
Fax: (0171) 495-7351

Executive Chef: Willi Elsener
Maître d'/Manager: Michael Difiore

THE GRILL ROOM
The Savoy
The Strand
London, England WC2R 0BP
Tel: (0171) 836-4343
Fax: (0171) 240-6040

Maître Chef: David Sharland
Maître Chef de Cuisine: Anton Edelmann
Maître d': Angelo Maresca
Manager: Angelo Maresca

Architecture: Beattes & Young

THE GRILL ROOM
Windsor Court Hotel
300 Gravier Street
New Orleans, Louisiana 70130
Tel: (504) 523-6000
Fax: (504) 596-4513

Chef: Jeff Tunks
Maître d': Kenneth Bryant

Architecture: Morris Aubry Associates
Restaurant Design: Frank Nicholson, F.N. Inc.

THE HASSLER ROOF RESTAURANT
Hotel Hassler Villa Medici
Piazza Trinità Dei Montl 6
Rome, Italy 00187
Tel: 6782651
Fax: 6789991

Executive Chef: Stuart Partridge

Architecture/Restaurant Design: Hans-Peter Karch

KABLE'S
The Regent Sydney
199 George Street
Sydney, NSW, Australia 2000
Tel: (238) 0000
Fax: (251) 2851

Chef: Serge Danserau
Manager: Renato Fabbro

Restaurant Design: Chhada Siembieda & Associates

LA MER
Halekulani
2199 Kalia Road
Honolulu, Hawaii 96815
Tel: (808) 923-2311
Fax: (808) 926-8004

Executive Chef: George Mavrothalassati
Maître d'/Manager: Jean-Yves Kervarrec

Architecture: Killingsworth, Stricker, Lindgren,
Wilson & Associates, Inc.
Restaurant Design: Terry/Egan Interiors

LA ROTONDE
Dolder Grand Hotel
Kurhausstrasse 65
Zurich, Switzerland 8032
Tel: (41) 1-251-62-31
Fax: (41) 1-251-88-29

Chef: George Angehrn
Maître d': Davide Giovannini
Manager: Henry J. Hunold

LAI CHING HEEN
The Regent Hong Kong
18, Salisbury Road, Tsim Sha Tsui
Kowloon, Hong Kong
Tel: (2721) 1211
Fax: (2739) 4546

Executive Chef: Cheung Kam Chuen
Manager: Simon Cheng

LE CHANTECLER
Hotel Negresco
37, Promenade des Anglais, B.P. 379
Nice, France 06007
Tel: (93) 16-64-00
Fax: (93) 88-35-68

Chef: Dominique Le Stanc
Maître d': Mr. Alain Harma
Manager: Michel Palmer

Restaurant Design: Madame Augier

LE CIRQUE
Mayfair Hotel Baglioni
58 East 65th Street
New York, NY 10021
Tel: (212) 794-9292
Fax: (212) 288-3730

Chef: Sylvain Portay
Pastry Chef: Jacques Torres

Restaurant Design: Ellen McClusky, McClusky &
Associates

LE GAVROCHE
Forty-Seven Park Street Hotel
43 Upper Brook Street
London, W1Y 1PF
England
Tel: 71-408-0881
Fax: 71-409-0939

Chef: Michel A. Roux
Maître d'/Manager: Silvano Giraloin

Restaurant Design: David Mlinark

LE GENTILHOMME
Le Richemond Geneve
8-10 Rue A. Fabri
1201 Geneva, Switzerland
Tel: 41-22-731-1400
Fax: 41-22-731-6709

Chef: Serge Labrosse
Maître d': Alain Guiget
Manager: Pierre Bord

LE LOUIS XV
Hôtel de Paris
Place du Casino
Monte Carlo, Monaco 98000
Tel: 92163001
Fax: 92166921

Chef: Alain Ducasse

Restaurant Design: Auge Pecoraro

LE MAROCAIN
La Mamounia
Avenue Bab Jdid
Marrakech, Morocco 40000
Tel: (212) 4-44-89-81
Fax: (212) 4-44-49-40

Head Chef: Bernard Guilhaudin
Moroccan Chef: Boujemaa Mars
Maître d': Retbi Mahiqub
Manager: Muttin Corrado

Architecture/Hotel Design: Henri Prost, Antoin Marchisio
Restaurant Design: Mr. Rho

LE RESTAURANT
The Regent Melbourne
25 Collins Street
Melbourne, Austrailia 3000
Tel: (613) 9653-0000
Fax: (613) 9650-4261

Executive Chef: Wolfgang von Wieser
Maître d'/Manager: Jack Vanderhelm
General Manager: Rudy Markl

Architecture: I.M. Pei; Pei, Cobb, Freed & Partners
Restaurant Design: Robert Lym,
Pei, Cobb, Freed & Partners

LES AMBASSADEURS
HÔTEL DE CRILLON
10 Place de la Concorde
Paris, France 75008
Tel: (44) 71-16-16
Fax: (44) 71-15-02

Head Chef: Christian Constant
Maître d'/Manager: Laurant Vanhoegaerden

Restaurant Design: Sonia Rykiel

LES CÉLÉBRITÉS
Essex House
155 West 58th Street
New York, New York 10019
Tel: (212) 484-5113
Fax: (212) 484-4680

Chef: Christian Delouvrier
Maître d'/Manager: Pierre Tagournet

LES SAISONS
Imperial Hotel
1-1, Unisaiwai-cho 1-chome, Chiyodi-ku
Tokyo 100
Japan
Tel: (03) 3504-1111
Fax: (03) 3581-9146

Chef: Hideki Kobayashi
Maître d': Nobuyuki Motoyoshi
Manager: Kojiro Muroya

Restaurant Design: Ferré-Duthilleul
Ogawa Ferré-Duthilleul Decoration

LESPINASSE
The St. Regis
2 East 55th Street at Fifth Avenue
New York, NY 10022
Tel: (212) 753-4500
Fax: (212) 787-3447

Chef: Gray Kunz

Architecture: Brennan Beer Gorman/Interiors,
Graham Design
Restaurant Design: Brennan Beer Gorman/Architects

THE MANSION ON TURTLE CREEK
RESTAURANT
The Mansion on Turtle Creek
2821 Turtle Creek Boulevard
Dallas, TX 75219
Tel: (214) 559-2180
Fax: (214) 528-4187

Executive Chef: Dean Fearing
Maître d': Wayne Broadwell
Manager: Jeff Trigger

Architecture: Hirsch/Bedner & Associates
Restaurant Design: Vision Design

MARK'S RESTAURANT & BAR
The Mark
Madison Avenue at East 77th Street
New York, New York 10021
United States

Chefs: Erik Maillard, Philippe Boulot
Maître d': John Squadrille
Manager: Hans Brand

Architecture: Peter Pennoyer,
Peter Pennoyer Architects Inc.
Restaurant Design: Mimi Russell, Mimi Russell Inc.

MASA'S
Vintage Court Hotel
650 Bush Street
San Francisco, CA 94108
Tel: (415) 989-7154
    (800) 258-7694
Fax: (415) 989-3141

Executive Chef: Julian Serrano
Maître d'/ General Manager: James Soule

Restaurant Design: Joel Hendler, Hendler & Hendler

ORANGERIE
Hotel Nassauer Hof
Kaiser-Friedrich-Platz 3-4
D-65183 Wiesbaden, Germany
Tel: (49) 611-1330
Fax: (49) 611-133632

Head Chef/Manager: Harald Schmitt
Chefs: Klaus Weingartz, Andreas Haugg
Maître d': Antoni de Rinaldis

Restaurant Design: Ilse v. Beckh, Jutta Babock,
Bàrbl Kàchele

THE ORIENT EXPRESS
Taj Palace Hotel
2, Sardar Patel Marg, Diplomatic Enclave
New Delhi, India 110021
Tel: 3010404
Fax: (011) 3011252

Executive Sous Chef: Shivanand Kain

Restaurant Design: Ms. Elizabeth Kerkar
Indian Hotels Company Ltd

PIERROT
Mandarin Oriental
5 Connaught Road, Central
Hong Kong
Tel: (852) 2522-0111
Fax: (852) 2810-6190

Chef: Peter Find
Maître d'/Manager: Philippe Bru

Restaurant Design: Cowperthwaite & Partners

PLUME
The Regent Hong Kong
18, Salisbury Road, Tsim Sha Tsui
Kowloon, Hong Kong
Tel: (2721) 1211 ext. 2256
Fax: (2739) 4546

Chef de Cuisine: Hubertus Cramer
Manager: Matthew Siegal

POSTRIO
The Prescott Hotel
545 Post Street
San Francisco, California 94102
Tel: (415) 776-7825
Fax: (415) 776-6702

Executive Chefs: Wolfgang Puck,
Mitchell & Steven Rosenthal
Pastry Chef: Janet Rikala
Maître d': Maureen Donegan

Restaurant Design: Pat Kuleto, Pat Kuleto Restaurants

RELAIS DU PARC
Le Parc Hotel
55/57, avenue Raymond-Poincare
Paris 75116
France
Tel: (01) 44-05-66-66
Fax: (01) 44-05-66-00

Head Chef: Gilles Renault
Director/Consulting Chef: Joël Robuchon
Maître d': Thierry Rouault

Restaurant Design: Ferré Duthilleul,
Ogawa Ferré Duthilleul Decoration

THE RESTAURANT AT HOTEL BEL-AIR
Hotel Bel-Air
701 Stone Canyon Road
Los Angeles, California 90077
Tel: (310) 472-1211
Fax: (310) 471-6267

Chef: Gary Clauson
Maître d'/Manager: Fernand Poitrois

Restaurant Design: Jerry Beale
Wilson & Associates

RESTAURANT DANIEL
Surrey Hotel
20 East 76th Street
New York, NY 10021
Tel: (212) 288-0033
Fax: (212) 737-0612

Chef: Daniel Boulud
Maître d': Bruno Jamais
Manager: David Newlin

Restaurant Design: Marc Palmer
Marc Palmer Interiors

RESTAURANT HAERLIN
Hotel Vier Jahreszeiten
Neuer Jungfernstieg 9-14
20354 Hamburg
Germany
Tel: (49) 40-34-94-0
Fax: (49) 40-34-94-602

Chef: Günther Harms
Manager: Alfred Mrugalska

RESTAURANT PETRUS
Island Shangri-La
Pacific Place, Supreme Court Road, Central
Hong Kong
Tel: (852) 2877-3838
Fax: (852) 2521-8742

Leese Robertson Freeman Designers Ltd.
Chef: Gérard Cavuscens
Maître 'd/Manager: Eric Desgouttes

Architecture: Wong & Ouyang (HK) Ltd
Restaurant Design: Paul Leese

SEA GRILL J. LE DIVELLEC
Radisson SAS Royal Hotel
Rue du Fosse aux Loups 47
Brussels 1000

Executive Chef: Yves Mattagne
Maître d': Alain Royer
Manager: Marc Meremans

Architecture/Restaurant Design: Nicolas Lecompte

ST. GIORGIO
Hotel Cipriani
Giudecca 10
Venezia, Italy 30133
Tel: (041) 520-77-44
Fax: (041) 520-39-30

Chef de Cuisine: Renato Piccolotto
Maître d's: L. Pradissito, M. Ossena
Manager: Dr. Natale Rusconi

Architecture/ Restaurant Design: Architect Gerard Gallet
Cabinet de M. Gallet

TRUFFLES
Four Seasons Hotel Toronto
21 Avenue Road
Toronto, Ontario, Canada M5R 2G1
Tel: (4126) 928-7331
Fax: 964-2301

Executive Chef: Denis Jaricot
Chef: Xavier Deshayes
Maître d'/Manager: Norman Hardie

Architecture: Houston Construction
Restaurant Design: Rosalie Wise Sharp

VERANDAH
Villa d'Este
Via Regina 40, 22012 Cernobbio
Lake Como, Italy
Tel: (31) 3481
Fax: (31) 348844

Chef: Luciano Parolari
Maître d': G. Rizzi
Manager: Marco Sorbellini

Architecture: Pellegrino Pellegrini di Valsolda

YÜ
The Regent Hong Kong
18 Salisbury Road, TsimShaTsui
Kowloon, Hong Kong
Tel: (2721) 1211
Fax: (2739) 4546

Executive Chef: Jürg Blaser
Chef: Man Kam Hing
Manager: Josef Schmid, Jr.

index

acknowledgments

Whenever I needed a tip on how to proceed writing about a grand dining room or an exceptional chef, David S. Wexler always cut through excess verbiage and pointed out what was really special about a place or person. Having spent 25 years as publisher of a highly successful restaurant magazine, *Restaurants & Institutions*, and since 1969 having guided *HOTELS* magazine from its beginnings with its redoubtable founder, Fergus McKeever, David is specifically qualified to understand the Great Hotel Restaurants everywhere on the globe.

In the 18 countries where the Great Hotel Restaurants are located... Thanks to all the hotels' general managers for their cooperation and enthusiasm and for their generosity in furnishing the fine photography. Also, at those same hotels, the chefs, food & beverage directors, restaurant managers and other staff deserve a large vote of thanks for providing all the detailed information, the menus, translations, and background information. These tireless people all gave me the material on which the book is based.

In the offices of *HOTELS* magazine in Des Plaines, Illinois... Don Lock, *HOTELS'* publisher at Cahners Publishing, deserves our applause for his idea of recognizing Ten Great Hotel Restaurants annually, and for recommending that I write the series and the book.

In PBC International's publishing offices... A big thanks goes to Deby Harding who edited this book and is one of the finest editors with whom I've ever worked. The project editor, Frank Zanone, was a strong teammate, always very helpful in keeping track of all fifty restaurants. For the handsome layouts I thank KC Witherell, a talented designer and Richard Liu, the technical director who supervised the stunning graphic effects. (I especially appreciate them because they made enough room for my copy.) To Mark Serchuck, publisher and Penny Sibal, managing director I thank for inviting me to write this book. Also thanks to Susan Kapsis, managing editor, to Naum Kazhdan for additonal photography, and special thanks to Dorene Evans who so efficiently helped me contact all of our hotels initially.